CORNWALL

—AT—

WAR

1939–1945

CORNWALL
— AT —
WAR
1939–1945

PETER HANCOCK

HALSGROVE

First published in Great Britain in 2002

British Library Cataloguing-in-Publication Data
A CIP record for this title is available from the British Library

ISBN 1 84114 161 5

HALSGROVE

Halsgrove House
Lower Moor Way
Tiverton, Devon EX16 6SS
Tel: 01884 243242
Fax: 01884 243325
email: sales@halsgrove.com
website: www.halsgrove.com

Printed and bound in Great Britain by Bookcraft (Bath) Ltd, Midsomer Norton

CONTENTS

DEDICATION

To the memory of Sergeant Pilot Walter Amos (1920–1942)

Killed when his Wellington Bomber was shot down over the North Sea.

Walter Amos.   MRS. I HANCOCK

PREFACE

Everyone who lived through the Second World War has their own story to tell. For this reason a book such as this cannot claim to be a comprehensive record of events, even in just one county. By its very nature it is also the story as told by the survivors. Clearly one has to be on guard against errors or embellishments after events have had sixty years or more to foment in the memory.

As I wrote this a sense of urgency developed, as surviving veterans succumbed to old age. Long-neglected coastal defences had collapsed or were slipping over the edge of cliffs, such as those at Spit near Par or at Charlestown. Elsewhere, they were being removed on grounds of safety, like part of the anti-tank wall at Kennack Sands on the Lizard, or had been obliterated immediately after the war, as at St Catherine's Fort, Fowey. Fortunately the realisation of their historical importance is slowly dawning and this has saved a few important sites, but only after decades of being overlooked. The Half Moon Battery at Pendennis, Falmouth, has been restored, as have 'The Tunnels' at the Cable and Wireless Station at Porthcurno. These impressive structures are now open to the public. More common is the prevailing belief that events between 1939 and 1945 are not yet history, and do not warrant particular attention. Only the passage of time, along with a review of the past, will see a change in this perception.

The operations that were carried out from Cornish airfields during the war have been well documented in various books and pamphlets, so I shall focus on some of the more unusual aspects, such as the use of FIDO and photographic reconnaissance at St Eval or ferrying operations from RAF Portreath.

I am indebted to a number of people and organisations who have allowed me to include photographs in this book. Whilst every effort has been made to secure permission, if there has been a failure to acknowledge anyone I offer my apologies.

Finally, it should be noted that the mention of various sites in this book does not infer that they are necessarily open to the public. Further enquiries should be made before making a visit.

ACKNOWLEDGEMENTS

I wish to thank the following for providing information during the compilation of this book:

N. Amy; F.R. Andrew of the Cornish Aviation Society; R.A. Bedingfield; J. Breslin of The Landmark Trust; the Cornish Studies Library, Redruth; the staff of the Courtney Library, Royal Cornwall Museum, Truro; County Libraries at Bodmin, Newquay, Redruth, St Austell and Truro; P.S. Evetts; R.C. Extence; P. Ferruccio; D. Flew; W.A. Frazier; F. Harper; A.V. Heggie; N. Hill of Eden Camp, Malton, North Yorkshire; The HMT *Lancastria* Association; Imperial War Museum; M. Lyne; G. Mitchell; the Museum of Submarine Telegraphy, Porthcurno; P. Newman; R. Parry; the guides at Pendennis Castle, St Anthony Head Battery and Tregantle Fort; Perranporth Airfield Ltd; Public Records Office, Kew; R. Sandercock; T.C. Savage; J.M. Shapland; V. Simms; Simmons Aerofilms; J.A. Stephens; the manager and staff of Summer Lodge holiday camp, Whitecross; Ms L. Thomas of the City of Westminster Archives Centre; J. Tough of The Association of Dunkirk Little Ships; J. Underhay; R. West; The *West Briton* newspaper; The *Western Morning News* Co. Ltd.; and not least S. Butler and the staff at Halsgrove, my brother John for help with ICT, and my parents, Ivy and Wilfred, for their help and encouragement.

Without the generous support of the above the book would not have been written.

THE GEORGE ELLIS COLLECTION

The author and publisher extend particular thanks to Terry Knight, Principal Library Officer with Cornwall County Library Service, for his help in providing images from the Ellis Collection. Photographer George Ellis moved to Cornwall on the day war broke out in 1939, working at first for the *Cornish Guardian* but staying for over forty years operating his own photographic business. During that time he produced approximately 16 000 images, mostly using plate negatives. His photographs of the war years in Cornwall are unique, and those he created of farming scenes and characters, landscapes, local annual events, celebrity visits, village feasts and carnivals, and much more taken over the ensuing years, reveal a deep love of his adopted homeland. They featured regularly in the local press and occasionally the nationals, as well as in his own picture postcards and calendars. The Cornish Studies Library acquired this truly remarkable collection in the early 1980s and now stores them in controlled conditions at its recently opened Cornwall Centre/Kresenn Kernow in Redruth.

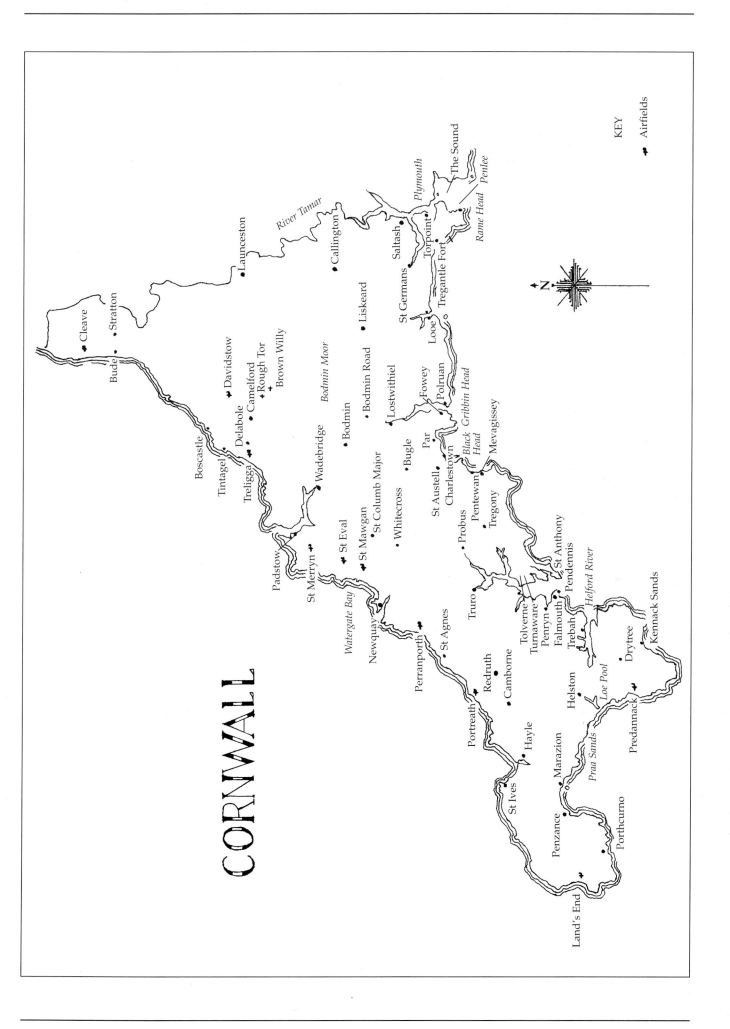

CORNWALL

KEY
Airfields

Land's End
Porthcurno
Penzance
St Ives
Marazion
Praa Sands
Hayle
Portreath
Redruth
Camborne
Helston
Loe Pool
Predannack
Drytree
Kennack Sands
Trebah
Falmouth
Penryn
Turnaware
Tolverne
Helford River
St Anthony
Pendennis
Truro
St Agnes
Perranporth
Newquay
Watergate Bay
Padstow
St Merryn
St Eval
St Mawgan
St Columb Major
Whitecross
Bodmin
Wadebridge
Boscastle
Tintagel
Treligga
Delabole
Camelford
Rough Tor
Brown Willy
Davidstow
Bodmin Moor
Cleave
Bude
Stratton
Launceston
River Tamar
Callington
Liskeard
St Germans
Saltash
Plymouth
The Sound
Penlee
Rame Head
Tregantle Fort
Torpoint
Looe
Polruan
Fowey
Lostwithiel
Bodmin Road
Bugle
Par
St Austell
Charlestown
Black Gribbin Head
Head
Pentewan
Mevagissey
Probus
Tregony

N

9

THE ROAD TO WAR

How horrible, fantastic, incredible it is that we are digging trenches and trying on gas-masks here because of a quarrel in a far away country between people of whom we know nothing.

NEVILLE CHAMBERLAIN [1]

The mood of much of Britain in the decade preceding the war was one of optimism. Many considered that it was unlikely that there would be another conflict. After all, the world was only now recovering from the Great War, the 'war to end all wars'. Pessimists looked with foreboding as Italy and Germany in turn became dictatorships, Spain disintegrated into civil war, and in the Far East, China was brutally invaded by Japan. These events were brought to the public's attention in Cornwall via radio, newspapers and news-reel reports in the cinemas.

Paradoxically, while the country might have been ill-prepared militarily for hostilities, schemes for organising the civilian population were already in place. Plans had been made for the evacuation of mothers and children as early as 1934, while the Government had set up the Food (Defence Plans) Department in 1936 to organise the supply of food and control prices should the country find itself at war.

An amazing story has only recently come to light which exposes the danger at this time of complacency and sees Cornwall playing host to an eminent Nazi. It has been told by Mr Michael Lyne, grandson of Alfred Browning Lyne, who founded the *Cornish Guardian* newspaper. He related how one day in 1938 his grandfather said to him, 'Michael, you are coming with me today. You will see history being made.' [2] His grandfather drove him in his American Stutz to Trengwainton House near Penzance. Here he met none other than Joachim von Ribbentrop, German Ambassador in London, before he became Foreign Minister. He was apparently friends of the Bolitho family and liked to take cliff walks during visits to them. Arriving on the Cornish Riviera express, he would be collected from the station in a large Mercedes Benz with whitewall tyres.

Mr Lyne, then a boy of eleven or twelve years of age, was introduced to Ribbentrop and politely shook hands, before being told to go and look at the fish in a big pond. Later at lunch the polished mahogany table with silver service made a lasting impression on him.

Following his private meeting with Ribbentrop, Mr Lyne senior said nothing on the return journey until they had passed Hayle. Clearly agitated, he eventually exclaimed, 'The arrogance of the man!' His grandson recalls his explanation, 'He said when Hitler has won world domination, Cornwall and St Michael's Mount will be given to Ribbentrop.' [3]

This episode may shed light on Germany's post-war intentions, suggesting that those advocating appeasement were misguided. It also indicates that Hitler and his Nazi supporters had designs on the British Isles at least as early as 1938 and possibly reveals what was in store once the Fuehrer had satisfied his ambitions in eastern Europe.

An interesting postscript to Mr Lyne's story occurred at the end of the war when, as a CO's driver, he was asked if he would like to spend a week doing guard duty at the Nuremberg Trials. Once there he told the guard commander that he knew Ribbentrop. His story was checked with the *Daily Mail* in London, and then he was allowed to renew his acquaintance. He recalled that before he entered the small cell he was told not to shake hands with the fallen Nazi. At first Ribbentrop didn't remember him, but on hearing the story, recalled his meeting with the young lad eight years before. He held out his hand, but Mr Lyne ignored the gesture. As sarcastically as he could he pointed out that the German had failed to gain St Michael's Mount. 'Things did not work out as planned,' came the reply. [4]

On becoming Prime Minister in May 1937 Neville Chamberlain had opened negotiations with Hitler, and in November Lord Halifax had been sent to Berchtesgaden, Hitler's retreat in the Bavarian Alps, to meet him face to face. So began a policy of appeasement and Chamberlain himself would meet Hitler on three occasions to try to satisfy his demands. On 4 February 1938, the day that Hitler took over the Supreme Command of the German Army, Ribbentrop, the belligerent adherent of the Fuehrer, became Foreign Minister. By 29 September 1938 Chamberlain, in a last-ditch effort to try to settle peaceably German claims to Czechoslovakia, was attending a four-power conference in Munich. He returned to Britain with his famous piece of paper on which was written, 'We, the German Fuehrer and Chancellor and the British Prime Minister, have had a further meeting... We regard the agreement signed last night and the Ango-German Naval Agreement as symbolic of the desire of our two peoples never to go to war with one another again.' [5] Triumphantly, yet naively, he declared 'Peace in our time'.

Chamberlain was also aware that the country was ill-prepared for war, and the Munich Agreement was buying him time. In September 1938 hundreds of thousands of reservists and Territorials had been mobilised. For example, the Redruth TA was dispatched to Southsea to help defend Portsmouth – until after the Munich crisis.

There was much debate about the Government's policy of appeasement, and by January 1939 serious doubts were being expressed about its efficacy. Mr John Foot, the prospective Liberal candidate for South East Cornwall Division, at a Liberal Party meeting in Bodmin chaired by Mr A. Browning Lyne, stated that war was inevitable if the country continued to retreat before the demands of Fascist dictators. He declared, 'We had seen during the last few weeks a complete collapse of the policy of appeasement and had instance after instance of the worthlessness of the promises given by Hitler and Mussolini.' [6] It was his opinion that the Government needed to stand up to these dictators before it was too late. If Britain was to defend the smaller countries that were under threat, 'we should be able to build up a great bulwark which the Fascist dictators would not dare to overthrow.' [7]

Most people hoped it would all blow over. In one newspaper report entitled 'A.R.P. Apathy' it was thought that, 'We ought to be doing a great deal more than we are in respect of air raid precautions.' [8] Three weeks later a meeting was held in Lostwithiel 'to consider the Government proposals for the evacuation of children from populous areas in the event of war.' However, 'The Mayor... remarked that although they had to carry out the scheme [of making a survey of every house in the borough] he hoped the occasion would never arise for putting it into operation.' [9]

Somewhat too late, a drive was made to expand the RAF. One newspaper report boasted that, '...since the air expansion programme began in 1935 vast opportunities have opened up for young men joining as Short Service Commission officers. There are approximately 7000 officers in the Royal Air Force today and nearly 4200 of them are holders of Short Service Commissions.' [10] The first surveys were conducted in 1937 to find possible sites for new airfields. Then, as late as 1939, the Emergency Powers (Defence) Act was passed which enabled the compulsory purchase of land for their construction or expansion.

On 24 October 1938 Ribbentrop proposed to the Polish Ambassador in Berlin that Danzig should be restored to the Reich, the episode that would trigger Britain's involvement in a fresh contest with Germany.

It is perhaps surprising in the light of future events that the German battleship, *Schleswig Holstein*, paid two courtesy visits to Falmouth; one in 1938, and one as late as early summer 1939. She was one of a small number of obsolete, pre-Dreadnought vessels that the Germans were allowed to keep under the terms of the Treaty of Versailles, and at over 14 000 tonnes, armed with four 11-inch and fourteen 6.7-inch guns, and being capable of reaching 18 knots, was one of the most powerful (until Hitler defied the ban, building the *Bismarck* and *Tirpitz* at over 42 000 tonnes). At the time she was used as a cadet training vessel, and the arrival of the immaculately dressed crew in Falmouth was no doubt a Nazi propaganda exercise. Of greater significance, the *Schleswig Holstein* was to fire the opening shots in the Second World War.

The Schleswig Holstein *adorned with Nazi emblem on her stern and flying a swastika, during a courtesy visit to Falmouth in 1938.*

WESTERN MORNING NEWS

She arrived in the disputed city of Danzig, Poland, in the last week of August 1939 on another so-called friendly visit, to commemorate the Germans who had fallen there during the First World War. However, without warning, at 4am on 1 September her 11-inch guns opened fire on the military installations on the Westerplatte, at the entrance to Danzig harbour. This bombardment opened the way for the subsequent German invasion. Two days later, Britain, followed by France, entered the war in support of

Poland. As for the *Schleswig Holstein*, the RAF bombed and sank her in December 1944.

Storm clouds had been gathering for some time. While people hoped peace would prevail, preparations for war had been gathering pace. On the eve of war it was reported under the headline 'St Austell's Intensive ARP Effort', that:

> The assembling and distribution of gas masks in the St Austell urban district has been completed, except for a few people who either were not fitted some months ago or who failed to attend one or other of the centres at which the masks have been distributed this week. [11]

Meanwhile in Bodmin, 'over 3000 of them had been issued to the public who had been lectured on how to use them and what the county town's preparations were in the event of an air raid.' [12] A week later, by which time war had been declared, the newspaper was able to report that:

> In addition to A.R.P. preparations, other steps had been taken. Housewives, whilst avoiding food hoarding, had made judicious extra provision, particularly of tinned goods, and people generally had done what was possible to meet a situation which had been feared must arise. [13]

The county waited with bated breath. When would the first air raid occur? Which town would be attacked first? Would there be gas attacks? Time passed but nothing happened. In Cornwall war still seemed a long way off, and life carried on much as normal during what became known as the 'Phoney War'. By November 1939 Mr A. Browning Lyne warned in his editorial in the *Cornish Guardian* that there was a '…danger of thinking the war was over before it had really begun.' [14] He urged people not to relax their guard, and in the meantime recognised that air supremacy was vital. A week later he commented wryly, 'Surely there never was such a war as this one. Are we really winning a war at all, or is it winning a peace?' [15]

However, by May 1940, the intrusion of external events could no longer be ignored by the general public. Some had joined the British Expeditionary Force (BEF) in the attempted defence of France. As the German Blitzkrieg swept west the BEF and hundreds of refugees were forced to follow an escape corridor to the beaches of Dunkirk. All the way they were harried by JU87 Stukka dive-bombers.

Extracts from a letter sent to a Penryn businessman by a Belgian industrialist were printed in the *Royal Cornwall Gazette* on 12 June 1940:

> The distraught people on the roads were tracked down by aeroplanes, which dived down to drop their chains of bombs relentlessly upon us. There were bodies of civilians on all roads and unspeakable tragedies – a man whose wife was killed at his side; a woman whose two children were killed near her, and many others.

Such reports must have scared the Cornish people and made them realise how close the realities of war really were.

The famous flotilla of little ships sent across the English Channel during *Operation Dynamo* helped to rescue 308 491 allied troops between 26 May and 3 June. [16] Miraculously the Channel was uncharacteristically calm. The vessels included four decrepit harbour tugs from Falmouth [17] and the fishing vessel *Leader* from Fowey. According to an Admiralty communiqué issued on 3 June, a total of 222 British naval vessels and 665 other British craft took part in the operation, aided by French naval and merchant ships. A Small Craft Registration Order that provided details of the boats available, helped to facilitate the operation.

One of the little ships, the Guide of Dunkirk, *now* Girl Guide, *in John Moor's boatyard, Mevagissey. Bought by the Girl Guides Association, after its unexpected call-to-arms it served as Cadgwith lifeboat until 1963.*

It was seen as a triumph by the propagandists, rather than an inglorious retreat. The official Admiralty communiqué published in the local papers said:

Its success is a triumph of Allied sea and air power in the face of the most powerful air forces which the enemy could bring to bear from air bases close at hand. [18]

Cornishmen caught up in the evacuation might have seen it differently. The *Royal Cornwall Gazette* reported on 5 June that Corporal Terence Larcombe, aged thirty-six, of Carclaze, St Austell, 'was in the retreat to the Channel ports. With other soldiers he was bombarded as they lay in a ditch, his foot was shattered and his comrade died in his arms. He crawled a quarter of a mile before he was picked up and taken to England on a trawler.' He had found sanctuary in a churchyard where he had spoken to a Frenchman, but sensing he couldn't trust him had moved on. [19] Many of the French in Northern France considered the English were deserting them. Yet the Pioneer Corps found French positions dug out, but no-one remained there. [20]

In the same report it mentioned that Private Harry Golley, aged twenty-two, of Bridges, Luxulyan, had reached England unscathed after '"a hell of a time" in Flanders.' [21]

On 12 June it was reported that Sergeant Thomas Savage, aged thirty, of St Austell, '…waited three days on the beach at Dunkirk without food, and finally escaped with only his rifle left of his equipment.' [22] In fact, nearly all the weapons, vehicles and heavy equipment were abandoned on the beaches. Mr Savage recalls being without food for a total of eight days. The Pioneers sergeant was eventually picked up after midnight by a Thames Hopper Barge,

Sergeant Savage; Rome, 1945.

MR T.C. SAVAGE

W24, having sheltered from bombs, shrapnel and flying flakes of stone thrown up from the harbour. He was taken to Margate where he received a bun and a cup of tea, and was given cards to write home, before being sent to Doncaster to re-form. The WVS finally provided him with a meal at Doncaster Racecourse – but only after the woman serving him defied an officer who wanted attention first. By the time he was eventually granted forty-eight hours leave he was in Wales! Mr Savage went on to fight in Malta and Italy, where he was wounded. [23]

A postcard sent by Sergeant Savage from Margate on 31 May, reassuring his wife of his safe return.

MR T.C. SAVAGE

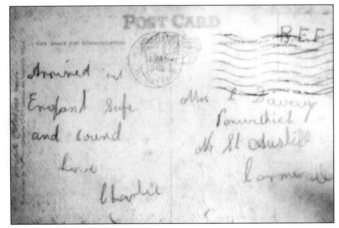

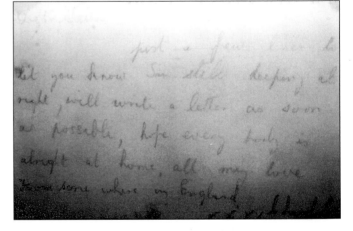

The message home. Note the BEF 'stamp' (above). Another card home, 'From some- where in England' (above right).

MR T.C. SAVAGE

A week later it was reported that a wounded corporal escaped 'from his captors, first by "borrowing" a Nazi motor cycle and on the second occasion an abandoned lorry.' He reached Dunkirk, but, '…for twenty-four hours he lay stretcher-bound on the beach under enemy fire awaiting embarkation.' [24]

None of the servicemen evacuated in *Operation Dynamo* or *Operation Cycle* – from St Valery and Le Havre between 10–13 June – landed in Cornish ports. However, during *Operation Aerial* between 15–25 June, which was responsible for the final evacuations from France and the Channel Islands, 16 971 British and 2654 Allied servicemen were landed in Falmouth, along with 14 units of mechanical transport. [25] Residents remember the harbour and Carrick Roads being packed with vessels. These included British, Dutch, Belgian and Polish cargo ships and passenger liners, as well as fishing vessels returning with troops from Nantes, St Nazaire, Brest, Cherbourg and St Malo. Not all of them made it; several vessels were lost, while those that had been immobilised joined the equipment abandoned on the beaches. Once ashore the 7th (Home Defence) Battalion of the DCLI helped to feed and process the arrivals, as well as taking charge of any weapons and provisions that were brought back.

At 4.30 on the morning of 15 June the skippers and crew of the Looe fishing fleet had only just turned in when, 'They were roused by the police, and told to get their crafts ready for a long sea trip, and to take on stores for a certain number of days.' [26] Soon there were scenes of, '…petrol and paraffin being loaded into the holds; women flying to and fro with huge pasties and square biscuit tins packed with saffron cakes and other eatables; oilskins, buckets, and other articles…' [27] Crowds of people packed the quayside as the fishing vessels *John Wesley, Iris, Our Girls, Our Daddy, Our Boys, Emma, Manxman* and *Talisman* set off. They sailed for Plymouth where they moored up at the Barbican basin awaiting further instructions. The fishermen wondered if they would be paid, and there was much talk of their final destination, with suggestions ranging, 'from Harfleur to Le Havre, down to Brest and Bordeaux, while one of the crueller wits thought that possibly we might be taking French officials away from Portugal.' [28]

They were signed on, after which they were under Navy rules and regulations. Then they were issued with steel helmets, service masks and rifles. 'Rumours were rife… One minute we were leaving directly, and the next we were to go home in two hours.' [29] In the event, the latter proved to be the case, and they returned to Looe on 19 June after four days of standing by. As they rounded the Banjo once more they could see crowds on the quay waiting to greet them; this time they included evacuee children who had arrived whilst they were away.

On 17 June the worst disaster in British maritime history occurred when the 16 243 ton Cunard/White Star liner HMT *Lancastria* was sunk at St Nazaire shortly after evacuees had been transferred to her. At 15.50 attacking Dornier Do17s scored direct hits with four bombs, one falling down the funnel. According to the Captain's report [30] 5200 evacuating troops and refugees were on board, and of these 2723 tragically lost their lives. Most of the 2477 survivors [31] who were rescued by nearby craft were taken to Plymouth. Some arrived in Falmouth on 19 June; 'Men, all sailors and soldiers, blackened and coated with oil, like the sea birds where oil fuel has been discharged.' [32]

One person observed, 'the gardener's wife and some houses near offer baths in turns.' [33] Then they were given fresh clothes by the Missions to Seamen. The procedure was to check any passports they carried, fill in landing cards, give them a medical examination and furnish them with food and drink at a canteen.

Winston Churchill, fearing news of the disaster would upset public morale, placed a D-Notice on the tragedy, thereby suppressing news of the sinking, the deaths being attributed to the evacuation. Survivors were forbidden to mention the disaster under King's Regulations. The Official Secrets Act ensures that documents relating to the sinking of a ship which only had the capacity for 3000 people will not be released until 2040.

The war had come to Cornwall.

While most young, able-bodied men stoically prepared for war, others searched their consciences and questioned whether it was right to participate. On Saturday 2 March 1940 a Peace Pledge Union meeting was held in Truro. When Mr R. Burnett addressed the crowd a group of hecklers tore down his banner and upset the platform, bringing the meeting to a close. [34]

Lt. Col. H.M. Ervine-Andrews, the only person at Dunkirk to receive a VC. Whilst Captain in the 1st East Lancashire Regiment, accompanied by some volunteers with a Bren gun, he repelled a German assault from the thatched roof of a barn. He is seen here attending the annual dinner of the Cornwall Branch of the Dunkirk Veterans Association at Tremont Hotel, Newquay, in 1988.

MR. T.C. SAVAGE

'"Do you think it wrong to serve in a non-combatant way when the empire is threatened as it is at present?" was a question which Judge Wethered, Chairman of the South-Western Tribunal for Conscientious Objectors [Bristol] put to Robert James Berryman, aged twenty-five...' [35] of Tregony when he applied for exemption from military service on religious grounds. After saying no he was transferred to the military service register for non-combatant duties. It was stated that:

> Berryman said he had been a pacifist about seven years, but he had not joined the Peace Pledge Union because he thought that many members were often actuated by political or material reasons rather than conscientious (sic). [36]

Such views were reinforced by eminent people such as the vicar of St Austell, Canon E. Roberts, who considered that there had been too much free speech and criticised the Peace Pledge Union 'and others who held pernicious views.' [37]

Similar belligerent opinions were also held by A.L. Rowse. He gave a lecture at Falmouth on 'Who Hitler is' and described him as a criminal genius. He went on to say:

> Make no mistake, there can be no compromise with Hitler or the Nazis. Make peace with them and they will use it to complete their preparations to greater efficiency and catch us even more unprepared. [38]

These beliefs were shared with Churchill and many others, so ideas of peace or compromise were brushed aside as preparations for war continued apace.

CHAPTER 1 – REFERENCES

(PC = Personal Communication)
[1] Speech broadcast on 27 September 1938 and referring to Czechoslovakia.
[2] *Cornish Guardian*, 18 January 2001, p. 27.
[3] PC: Mr M. Lyne.
[4] Ibid.
[5] Imperial War Museum.
[6] *Cornish Guardian and Cornwall County Chronicle*, 26 January 1939, p. 5.
[7] Ibid.
[8] *Cornish Guardian and Cornwall County Chronicle*, 5 January 1939, p. 7.
[9] *Cornish Guardian and Cornwall County Chronicle*, 26 January 1939, p. 6.
[10] *Cornish Guardian and Cornwall County Chronicle*, 19 January 1939, p. 11.
[11] *Cornish Guardian and Cornwall County Chronicle*, 31 August 1939, p. 2.
[12] Ibid.
[13] *Cornish Guardian and Cornwall County Chronicle*, 7 September 1939, p. 3.
[14] *Cornish Guardian and Cornwall County Chronicle*, 9 November 1939, p. 7.
[15] *Cornish Guardian and Cornwall County Chronicle*, 16 November 1939, p. 9.
[16] Not the normally erroneously quoted figure of 338 226 – see *B.E.F. Ships before, at and after Dunkirk* (1999), John de S. Winser, p. 36.
[17] *Falmouth's Wartime Memories* (1994), Trelawny, p. 16.
[18] *Western Morning News*, 4 June 1940.
[19] PC: Mr T.C. Savage, recalling a conversation with Mr T. Larcombe.
[20] PC: Mr T.C. Savage.
[21] *Royal Cornwall Gazette*, 5 June 1940, p. 3.
[22] *Royal Cornwall Gazette*, 12 June 1940, p. 2.
[23] PC: Mr T.C. Savage.
[24] *Royal Cornwall Gazette*, 19 June 1940, p. 4.
[25] *B.E.F. Ships before, at and after Dunkirk* (1999), John de S. Winser, p. 51.
[26] *Cornish Guardian and Cornwall County Chronicle*, 27 June 1940, p. 8.

[27] Ibid.

[28] Ibid.

[29] Ibid.

[30] P.R.O., Kew ADM199/2133.

[31] The H.M.T. *Lancastria* Association.

[32] From the diary of Evelyn Radford, published in the *Cornish Review*, No. 4 (1967), p. 40.

[33] Ibid.

[34] *Royal Cornwall Gazette*, 6 March 1940, p. 8.

[35] *Royal Cornwall Gazette*, 5 June 1940, p. 4.

[36] Ibid.

[37] *Royal Cornwall Gazette*, 29 May 1940, p. 2.

[38] *Royal Cornwall Gazette*, 13 March 1940, p. 2.

THREAT OF INVASION: COASTAL DEFENCE

Bearing ourselves humbly before God, but conscious that we serve an unfolding purpose, we are ready to defend our native land against the invasion by which it is threatened. We are fighting by ourselves alone; but we are not fighting for ourselves alone.

CHURCHILL [1]

B y July 1940 Hitler had conquered France and the Channel Islands, and was determined to hold on to his newly acquired territories by all means possible. A so-called 'Atlantic Wall' was soon being constructed comprising massive concrete bunkers, gun emplacements and mine fields supported by underground hospitals and ammunition stores, making the Channel Islands the most heavily fortified region in western Europe. Yet at the time of the evacuation from Dunkirk in May, most Cornish beaches had still not been protected by barbed wire.

German coastal defences in Guernsey: part of Hitler's 'Atlantic Wall'.

Until that time Cornwall was out of range of German bombers and any danger lay far to the east. Now, all of a sudden, the enemy had access to captured French ports as well as airfields at Lorient, Vannes, Bordeaux-Merignac and Brest, putting the enemy little more than a hundred miles away across the Channel.

Cornwall now found itself on the frontline. Meanwhile across the Channel German troops, emboldened by their recent success, talked of the imminent occupation of Britain.

Historically, the expected destination of an invasion fleet has been the south coast. Long before the Spanish Armada, Henry VIII had a line of castles built from Pendennis to the Thames estuary because of a feared French invasion. It is therefore not surprising to find Second World War gun batteries beneath the Henrician fortifications at Pendennis and St Catherine's Castle, Fowey, augmented by scores of pillboxes, the majority facing bays and harbours on the south coast.

The Carrick Roads provided Penryn, Falmouth and Falmouth Docks with access to the English Channel. The entrance was protected by a submarine net which could be opened by a fishing vessel if it received the correct coded message. Gun batteries at Pendennis and St Anthony's Head, and augmented by another next to St Mawes Castle, provided protection against surface vessels and aircraft.

First constructed in 1793 to the south-east of Pendennis Castle's keep, the Half Moon Battery had been adapted over the years, and updated at the outbreak of hostilities when Fixed Defences Falmouth was upgraded from a Category B to a Category A port. The crescent-shaped battery was equipped with two new six-inch high-angle coastal defence guns by Royal Artillery reservists, and the original guns dating from the First World War were transferred to St Anthony Battery. They were partly enclosed by curved concrete walls and hidden at the front by camouflage netting. In December 1940 canopies were added as a precaution against air attacks following a recent raid on Falmouth. The two gun emplacements were linked by an underground magazine, and access to the whole complex from the main castle was via two tunnels running under the ramparts.

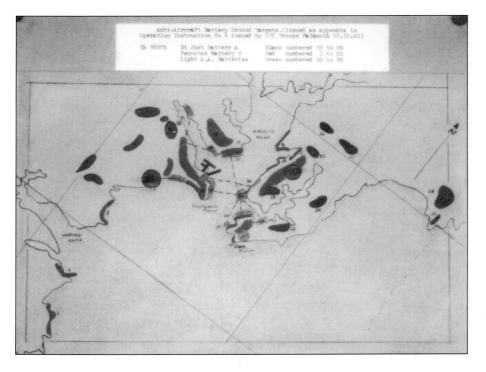

Anti-aircraft battery ground targets, as displayed on the information board of the BOP, Pendennis.

At night defence electric lights (DELs), mounted on concrete platforms above the rocks at Pendennis Point and Crab Quay, could be used to seek out the targets. Between the two sets of searchlights was a sunken engine room to provide them with power.

An anti-aircraft gun at Pendennis, facing out over the Carrick Roads.

Access to the subterranean Battery Plotting Room, Pendennis, with large ventilators protruding from the walls.

For a time the task of manning the guns was given to 201 Battery RA under the command of Major Stephens of Ponsanooth. About 100 men were divided equally between Pendennis and St Anthony Battery, after they had completed their training in Plymouth. Mr Victor Simms was a sergeant in the RA who served at both Pendennis and St Anthony. He feels they were adequately prepared to repel an invasion, and recalls helping to train on 'young infantry boys' at the batteries before 201 Battery was posted overseas. [2]

Running down the north coast were a series of radar stations. The most westerly of these included a military observation post built into the cairn at Chapel Carn Brea, overlooking Land's End Airport. These then continued up the south coast to Rame Head, and beyond. As an example, at Downderry four radio masts were located between the beach and the narrow coast road. The primary school and residential housing now cover the site.

All that remains of the radar station that once stood on the cliffs above Blackbottle Rock near Polruan.

If the enemy was detected by one of these radar stations the sighting and position would be radioed to the Fire Command Post at Pendennis. They would then alert the Battery Commanders at St Anthony Battery and St Mawes by telephone. The gun detachments, perhaps resting in the Victorian war shelter, would be alerted by an alarm bell.

The Battery Observation Post (BOP) was conveniently located in the salient of the south-facing bastion. Inside the steel door the walls of the retangular room were painted dark blue to maximise the view through the long, narrow observation window. Here ten personnel, men and women, worked together in cramped surroundings. Using a range of equipment they determined the current range and position of the enemy. In the centre of the room was a Watkins Depression Position Finder, a semi-circular table on which was mounted a telescope to track the target, linked in turn to equipment that would provide accurate gun settings. These were based on the target distance as well as taking into account tidal and weather conditions. A smaller Depression Range Finder was available for tracking close range, fast moving targets like MTBs. A Displacement Co-ordinate Converter was used to predict the future position of the targets. These were then relayed to the gun crew in Half Moon Battery using Magslip transmission equipment, a basic form of remote control. The Fire Commander co-ordinated the response with the guns at St Anthony Battery, as well as keeping in touch with the Battery Plotting Room next to the Bay Hotel in Falmouth by telephone.

The Battery Observation Post at Pendennis, seen from the guns, and behind that, the Tudor keep used for storing secret codes and plans. The letters on the wall label pegs used by the gun crew to hang their capes and gas masks.

The Battery. The original guns were decommissioned in 1945. This is a 1946 replacement, recently installed.

Meanwhile, in the underground magazine between the gun emplacements of Half Moon Battery, the ammunition was being prepared. Before the magazine crew descended the steps they had to use a boot scraper in a recess in the wall in order to remove any stones which might create a spark. Inside the steel doors the corridor had been covered by their Victorian predecessors with smooth, white ceramic tiles, again to avoid sparks being struck. Another precaution that continued into the twentieth century was for the men to first enter a changing room to change into magazine clothing made of cotton tied with braided cords, together with canvas slippers, thus discarding any metal belt buckles or buttons that could create a spark.

The cartridges and shells were kept in separate rooms. Each gun had its own cartridge and shell store with a capacity of 500 apiece. Being underground and well-ventilated, the magazine was kept at an almost constant temperature. The men were aware that if any of the explosive charges became unstable they emitted a peculiar marzipan-like smell. Special racks were constructed to hold the shells. Their weight depended on the type, there being shrapnel, armour piercing, or high explosive shells containing TNT. Receiving the order, the shells would be prepared, transferred to the gunners using a hoist and loaded.

The shell store of the magazine, adjacent to but separate from the cartridge store.

The cartridge store. Notice the cartridge cases, racks, shielded lights and the hatch into the shell store.

Now the Fire Commander could give the order to fire. The guns had a range of over 19km, so, depending on weather conditions, the target would often be out of sight.

Once fired, observers in the Battery Observation Post, as well as their counterparts at St Anthony, could use binoculars as well as radar signals to see if they had hit the target. A Time of Flight Indicator sounded a warning bell three seconds before the shells struck, and they would no doubt watch for tell-tale smoke. A report of the action would then be radio-telegraphed to Western Command as well as the Admiralty.

St Anthony Battery. The officers' quarters, now holiday cottages.

From such information received the details of four engagements were logged during the war. These occurred in February and April 1943 and February and March 1944. In each case the target was identified by radar at night. All were suspected E-boats at a range of 15 to 20km. There is no record of any enemy vessels being hit by one of the salvoes. This is not surprising when the targets were at extreme range and capable of moving rapidly from danger. Also, the time taken from the first radar plot being received to the first salvo being fired was from twenty-two minutes to an hour and a half! Then the bombardment lasted for ten to twenty minutes. There was also an incident when the guns fired across the bows of a 'friendly' vessel which had failed to provide the correct code to the fishing boat manning the submarine net.

St Anthony Battery was very similar to, and had the same facilities as Pendennis Battery. It was also subservient to the one at Falmouth and could only fire the guns if it received orders from the Fire Command Post at Pendennis. The battery had been in existence since the early years of the twentieth century and had been manned during the First World War. Since then it had been inspected regularly. At the outbreak of hostilities only the two 6-inch breech-loading guns had to be remounted. They were set in seven-foot deep gun emplacements, with a semi-circular sloping apron in front of them covered with natural Trinidadian lake asphalt. This durable material was also used on the roof of the BOP and can still be seen today.

The range finder post, St Anthony Battery.

St Anthony Battery BOP. The new reinforced steel joists were installed during its restoration in 1997, but it remains unglazed and empty, apart from a modern telescope.

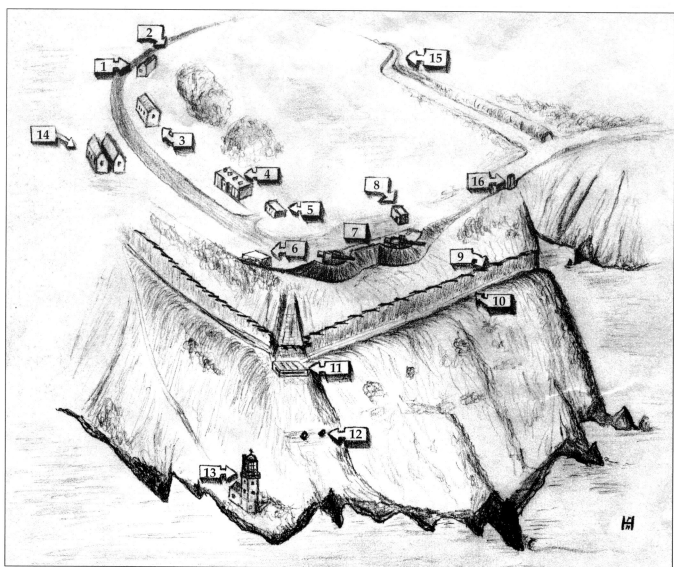

St Anthony Battery

1. Guard Room
2. Military Road
3. Canteen
4. Officers' Quarters
5. Armaments Artificers' Workshop
6. B/1 Gun Store
7. Two 6" Guns above Magazine
8. B/2 Gun Store
9. Unclimbable Fence
10. Rampart and Rock-Cut Ditch
11. Battery Observation Post (BOP)
12. Searchlights (DELs)
13. St Anthony Lighthouse
14. Barracks
15. Defensive Bank, Ditch and Wall
16. Rangefinder Post

As at Pendennis, the magazine was located beneath the gun emplacements, and was entered by descending steps to the 'magazine area'. This space enabled the ammunition to be lowered into the magazine using davits mounted on the wall, as well as providing a back-up system should the lifts to the guns fail. The ceiling of the magazine was barrel-vaulted in brick and the interior was laid out symmetrically in a broad H-shape. Entering the building the men went through the same safety procedures as at Pendennis, changing in the Shifting Lobby before being inspected by a guard who would then allow them to pass a barrier into the cartridge stores.

The entrance to the underground magazine. Notice the date, 1904, above the doorway (below left).

A warning inside the door of the battery, dated 1941 (below right).

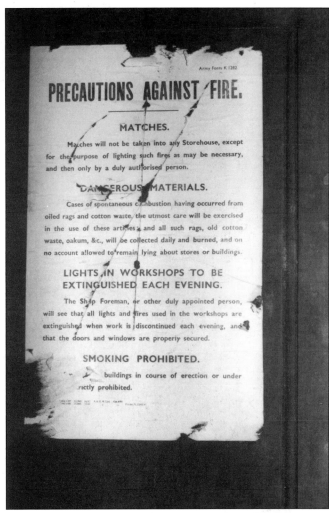

St Anthony Battery – The Magazine.

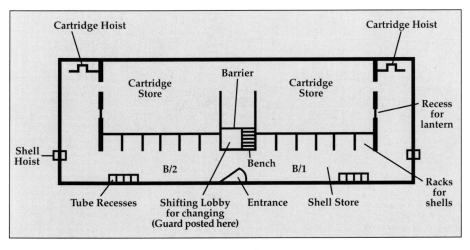

Inside the 'Filled Shell Store B/1' Note the vaulted brick ceiling and the remains of the racks for the shells.

The unrestored cartridge store, showing the alcoves for lights and the steel hatch providing access to the cartridge lift.

The cartridge lift. Note the hinged platform ready to receive the cartridge. This would be raised to a vertical position using the handle beneath it, so the cartridge can be winched by hand to the gun (B/1) above.

Each side of the magazine was responsible for its respective guns, B/1 and B/2. The front half of the magazine was used to store shells, half of which were kept on the floor with the rest on racks above them. On the outside wall was a blue/grey wooden box divided into compartments where the small firing tubes were kept until the shells were to be primed. (This is labelled A/1 and A/2 from a period when Pendennis Battery was being refurbished.)

Kept strictly separate, on the other side of a dividing wall, were the more unstable cartridges in cases. The number and type stored there varied depending on the requirements. [3] When they were needed they were passed through a hatch to a vertical cartridge hoist which delivered them to the guns. The shells had their own lift inclined to an angle of about 60 degrees. Both were manually cranked.

Each gun also had its own gun store behind the magazine. These, along with the guns, are the only elements of the battery that can no longer be seen.

The shell lift remains in remarkably sound condition. Only the ingress of rainwater from above prevents the chains which operate it from functioning.

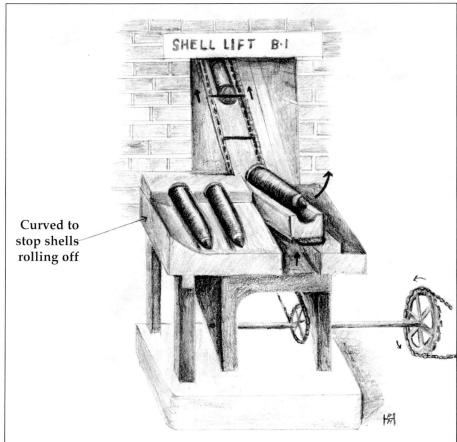

Curved to stop shells rolling off

The stone-cut ditch, ramparts and the remains of the unclimbable fence, all part of the improvements made in 1885.

The BOP was similar to its counterpart at Pendennis. Again, it was situated at the southern-most point of the ramparts. These followed the contours of the headland in roughly an L-shape and were further protected by a rock-cut ditch and a spiked steel fence angled out from the ramparts. The rear of the battery was more lightly protected by a ditch and embankment retained by a stone wall.

The third element in the defence of Falmouth was at St Mawes, where four guns were positioned on the hill to the north of the Henrician castle, mainly as a precaution against MTBs. Searchlights were also installed by the walls to the south of the castle.

A smaller and less impressive complex guarded the mouth of the River Fowey. Like Pendennis, St Catherine's Battery was built near the obsolete Tudor fort. A harbour boom protected the entrance to the river, with two 6-pounder guns nearby.

The battery was established between June and September 1940 and subsequently improved at various times. Two guns were installed, both 4.7-inch naval guns of 1917 vintage. No.1 Gun was mounted on the high ground overlooking the castle, while No.2 Gun was set in the seaward of the two granite gun emplacements above the rocks.

No.2 Gun Emplacement (on the right) at St Catherine's Fort, Fowey, facing across the mouth of the River Fowey towards Polruan where there was also a small battery on the promontory (above left).

The platform for No.2, 6 pounder gun, Fowey. This would have been just inside the harbour boom (above right).

Instructions were given to elaborately camouflage the guns using camouflage netting thickly garnished with vegetation. This was hung like a curtain from the concrete canopies over the guns using rings and a wire, so that the barrels poked out between them. The bottom of the netting was attached to 'tent pegs' by a length of cord tied with a quick-release knot. The granite slopes of No.2 Gun's emplacement were to be disguised with steel wool and sea weed! Even the Tudor keep received a shroud of garnished camouflage netting.

Each gun had its own ammunition store, and a Battery Observation Post was constructed and also well camouflaged. This originally faced inland, but the orientation was reversed when it was extended in 1943. At the same time a 40mm Bofors gun was set up nearby. The site now boasted a parade ground and training hut, a guard room and toilet block, as well as an engine room to power the searchlights. There was also a pillbox guarding the approach from the west of the fort, and beyond that a minefield in Allday's Field.

Pillboxes were the most prolific of coastal defences. Quickly constructed in strategic locations, they formed a sheltered observation platform and defensive position. Eight basic designs for pillboxes were drawn up in June and July 1940 by the Directorate of Fortifications and Works (FW3) at the War Office. This body had been set up in May of that year under the directorship of Major-General G.B.O. Taylor.

The site of the parade ground and training hut, St Catherine's Fort, Fowey (above left).

Concrete walls and steel window shutters of a war-time building contrast with the modern china-clay refinery at Spit, near Par (above right).

Pillboxes were designated FW3/22 through to 29, although the Type 28 was later enlarged, thus creating the FW3/28A. The specification of most of these included bullet and shrapnel protection, and in most cases basic blast walls to protect the entrances. Some, like the Type 28, were strengthened to be shell-proof. None were designed to provide living accommodation or any form of comfort for the occupants.

Standardised designs like these meant that certain components such as doors, lintels and loopholes could be pre-fabricated and the rectangular, square, hexagonal, octagonal or circular shapes could be created in concrete cast inside shuttering. There were variations according to the location and the materials available. Pillboxes in Cornwall were invariably built of concrete where sand and cement were readily available, while further up the south coast in Dorset bricks were used extensively.

The Type 22 Pillbox was a basic hexagonal structure designed as a look-out post that could be manned by riflemen. This is probably the most common type in Cornwall. The number of loopholes and their position depended on the specific location and topography. The square Type 23 had provision for a light anti-aircraft gun located in an open annex, while the Type 24 was hexagonal and was intended to be defended with rifles or light machine guns. The Type 25 or 'Armco' was small and circular, often being shuttered inside corrugated iron which left tell-tale vertical striations on the exterior. The Type 26 Pillbox was a simple square building with one doorway and loopholes in each wall. Often constructed near airfields, the Type 27 usually had one-metre thick walls and could be octagonal or hexagonal, incorporating a central well which

Coastal defences at Spit, near Par Harbour (above).

Coastal defence in Cornwall was in marked contrast to the German equivalent (see p.20): a Type 22 Pillbox built over a disused lime kiln at Polkerris, near Par (right).

could be used as a look-out or where a light AA gun might be located. Inside the rectangular Type 28s was a 2-pounder anti-tank gun, 6-pounder Hotchkiss gun or Vickers machine gun. The main identifying feature of this one is a large concrete table on which to mount the gun. The Type 29 was similar to the Type 24, but was provided with thicker walls. Despite these epithets, it appears that there was no attempt at conformity, and no hard and fast rules were laid down for their construction.

Guarding the entrance to Plymouth Sound was Penlee Battery. Facing east, it was built into the hillside of Rame Head, and like St Anthony Battery it had a rock-cut ditch and secure fence, while its rear was protected by earthen banks. It was armed with three 9.2-inch guns and two 6-inch guns. Originally

a 13.5-inch breech-loading gun weighing 67 tons was installed, but when it was tested it ran its bearings. The story goes that at that time the ditch was being filled in, so after it had been replaced with smaller guns the barrel was rolled into the ditch and buried. This may be true, but recent attempts to find it using metal detectors have so far failed. [4] Nearby was a radar station sited by the southern wall of St Michael's Chapel on Rame Head.

An attack on the north coast was considered unlikely. However precautions were taken, such as re-installing the guns at Battery near Padstow, to protect the mouth of the Camel Estuary.

Beaches that could be used for a landing were covered in obstacles constructed from barbed wire, scaffolding, tank traps and mines. Two interesting examples were at Loe Bar near Helston and Kennack Sands on the Lizard.

At Loe Bar the 75th Independent Infantry Brigade and Cornwall Coastal Area, which included The Sixth Battalion of the DCLI, constructed over half a kilometre of obstacles from convoluted scaffolding along the broad beach. In between this work they were undertaking training exercises, night patrols and mock battles, sometimes using live ammunition. Pillboxes were built on the cliffs either side of the bar, while the Loe – the largest fresh water lake in

Cornwall – was protected from enemy seaplanes by large timber booms as well as being mined. Penrose House overlooking the Loe was requisitioned as an army HQ.

At Kennack Sands an anti-tank wall was constructed behind the two beaches and defended with pillboxes linked by trenches. The wall was 1150mm thick and about two metres high, being constructed from two leaves of concrete blocks, infilled with large pebbles from the beach, mixed with mortar. Recently the unstable and dangerous wall behind West Kennack Sands was removed, along with most of the pillboxes. A Type 22 pillbox remains, largely hidden amongst the vegetation on the dunes.

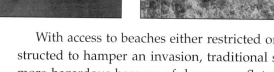

Penrose House, overlooking Loe Pool, was requisitioned by the army (above left).

Penlee Battery, Rame Head. The surviving seaward gun emplacement can just be seen above its magazine, hidden amongst the vegetation (above right).

With access to beaches either restricted or made difficult by obstacles constructed to hamper an invasion, traditional summer pursuits were now even more hazardous because of dangerous flotsam. Even the swimming pool in Penzance was fenced off and an anti-aircraft battery positioned there, manned by the army and the Home Guard.

In August 1941 warnings were published in the local newspapers against touching strange objects on beaches. 'Already a number of deaths and injuries have been caused by such objects being picked up or touched by the unwary,' it warned. [5] It must have seemed as if the county had changed for ever.

The anti-tank wall, East Kennack Sands. Notice the roof of a pillbox, right foreground.

The wall would have originally run the length of the beach. However, some sections were recently removed for safety reasons.

Almost hidden in the undergrowth stand these crumbling walls constructed to repel a powerful invader. These are at Spit near Par.

CHAPTER 2 – REFERENCES

(PC = Personal Communication)

[1] Winston Churchill in a BBC broadcast, London, 14 July 1940.

[2] PC: Mr V. Simms.

[3] PC: Mr A.V. Heggie, RA Master Gunner (ret.)

[4] PC: Mr J. Breslin of the Landmark Trust.

[5] *Royal Cornwall Gazette,* 6 August 1941, p. 2.

— **3** —

THREAT OF INVASION: CIVIL DEFENCE

If invasion comes, everyone – young or old, men and women – will be eager to play their part worthily. [1]

T he horrors of the Western Front had brought home the reality of modern warfare to most families in Britain. It also left them, and the authorities, with some expectation of what any fresh hostilities would involve. Technology, particularly in its application to aircraft and tanks, had moved on since the Great War, so any future conflict was unlikely to be bogged down in trench warfare but was expected to be more mobile. This would mean that it would involve the civilian population; it would be a people's war.

One of the ghastly aspects of the First World War had been the use of poison gas and there was no reason to suppose that the Germans would not make use of this weapon again. Therefore, as early as the Munich crisis in September 1938, 38 million gas masks had been issued. These came in a variety of types, some for adults in different sizes, others for children, and more specialised masks for civil defence personnel and the army. In March 1940 about 130 children's respirators and 110 protective helmets for babies were issued at Truro. [2] The little cardboard boxes which contained the respirators became a familiar sight as people were urged to carry them at all times. Small holes were punched through the top and bottom of the side panels so a string could be threaded through and underneath them to serve as a carrying strap.

The infamous gas mask. This one is in pristine condition, fortunately never having been required.

A leaflet issued by the Ministry of Home Security advised, 'Practise putting them on and get used to wearing them with confidence.' [3] Children were given similar instructions at school where their gas masks were also regularly inspected by an ARP officer. Pupils also practised working in their respirators to accustom themselves to wearing them.

The instructions for using the gas masks were conveniently printed inside the cover of the box, beginning with 'Packing of Respirator'. This stated that the 'heavy end' – the filter – should be inserted first and that 'the transparent eye-piece should lie evenly on the top of the container and at full length without any deformation.' The Government leaflet also advised: 'To prevent the face-piece misting over, smear a little soap lightly on the inside once a week.' Alternatively, 'No.2 Anti-gas ointment' was available from the chemist – price 6d. [4]

One of the many leaflets offering advice to the civilian population.

The instructions for using the respirator advised 'putting chin into facepiece and then draw the straps over the head. Adjust straps to obtain close but comfortable fit.' Obviously it was important to obtain an airtight seal between the rubber mask and the face. Unfortunately no-one at the time was aware of the danger of the asbestos which was used in the filters.

Two types of hazard were predicted, gas or vapour, and liquid blister gas. It was advised to remove any clothing that had been contaminated by the liquid before going inside to wash, for 'your health matters more than your

PACKING OF RESPIRATOR

PACKING OF RESPIRATOR

The respirator should be placed in box with heavy end (container) standing on bottom of box.

The transparent eyepiece should lie evenly on the top of the container and at full length without any deformation.

WHEN RESPIRATOR IS REQUIRED FOR USE

1. Hold Respirator by the straps.

2. Put on by first putting chin into the facepiece and then draw the straps over the head. Adjust straps to obtain close but comfortable fit.

3. Take off by pulling the straps over the head from the back. DO NOT TAKE RESPIRATOR OFF BY PULLING THE CONTAINER UPWARDS OVER THE FACE.

Instructions inside the lid of the little buff-coloured box of a 'respirator', more commonly referred to as a gas mask.

feelings.' If there was nowhere available to wash, the wardens or police 'will know where the public cleansing centres are.'[5] One such Decontamination Cleansing Station was constructed at Windsor Lane, Saltash. The purpose-built facility was constructed at a total cost of £729 16s 0d, including £79 10s 0d for the installation of the boiler and plumbing to provide hot water for the showers.[6]

Most people diligently took their respirators everywhere they went for a short time after the outbreak of war, but as gas attacks failed to materialise during the 'phoney war', they were soon discarded or forgotten. Taking the offensive, in 1939 The Army Anti-Gas School was opened at Tregantle Fort, where three-week training sessions in gas warfare took place. The Napoleonic fort itself, with its defences facing inland, was not considered important at this time.

It soon became clear that a greater danger would be from conventional bombs. In the summer of 1939 there was a big push to build public underground air-raid shelters. The public was also encouraged to build, or have constructed, their own air-raid shelter in the back garden. A Government-issued kit, known as an Anderson shelter after the Home Secretary, Sir John Anderson, was free to families earning less than £250 per annum, or could be purchased for about £7. For this, one received a collection of curved and straight corrugated steel sheets which, once erected and located in a pre-dug hole, created a shelter 6ft 6in long and 6ft high. Further protection could be afforded by piling earth over the roof – which could then be planted with vegetables. By September 1940 nearly a quarter of a million had been produced. Cold, dark and damp they may have been, but they undoubtedly saved many lives.

In 1941 a new indoor shelter was created that was like a steel mesh cage, the top of which could serve as a table. This was the Morrison shelter, named after the new Minister of Home Security, Herbert Morrison. Again they were successful in saving lives, as was noted after a raid on Falmouth on 25 November 1941; 'A Morrison table undoubtedly saved the life of a mother and her two small children on this occasion.'[7]

The Minister of Home Security was also responsible for air-raid wardens. The ARP Control Centre was established in the basement rooms on the eastern side of (old) County Hall in Truro. This was also the headquarters of Allied Civil Defence Services including the police, fire service and medical services, as well as the Gas Identification Service and Highways.

The County Air Raid Precautions Controller was Major George H. Johnstone. Under him were the Area Sub-Controllers. Most of the ARP wardens themselves were part-time and had responsibility for a particular area, where they became a familiar sight. Their role was to enforce black-out regulations and work alongside the rescue services if there was an air raid. There were regular reports in the local newspapers of people breaking the blackout restrictions, as it was feared that a tiny exposed light might be seen from an enemy plane. Again, the Ministry of Home Security was able to offer advice with a booklet entitled *Air Raids – What You Must Know. What You Must Do* for 3d.

A contemporary postcard showing that 'Dad's Army' was not the first to poke fun at the Home Guard or the solitary soldier left on guard duty. This one was sent to a person in St Columb on 4 April 1940. It was No.3 of the Camp Silhouette Series.

Helping the ARP wardens were members of the Women's Voluntary Service (WVS). This body had been founded in 1938 to involve women in civil defence work. They gave their spare time to provide food and drink to the forces and provide clothing for blitz victims, as well as help with anything else that was necessary. For example, members of the WVS assisted in the sergeants' mess at RAF St Mawgan. Typically, at St Stephen, the WVS held weekly knitting sessions to provide garments for the forces, as well as making pasties and other meals which were served at WVS centres. They were also taught self-defence, first aid and family nursing.

The civilian population also had to be made ready to resist any invasion. To this end a number of leaflets were issued by the Ministry of Information 'in co-operation with the War Office and the Ministry of Home Security.' In *If the Invader Comes*, printed in June 1940, the civilian population was urged not to be taken by surprise, as had happened in Europe:

> When Holland and Belgium were invaded, the civilian population fled from their homes. They crowded on the roads … and so helped the enemy by preventing their own armies from advancing against the invaders. You must not allow that to happen here.

Making the public aware of the enemy – spotting enemy uniforms.

It went on to list seven rules, including the order to 'stay put', not to believe rumours or spread them, and make sure the enemy could not get hold of any

If the
INVADER
comes

WHAT TO DO — AND HOW TO DO IT

THE Germans threaten to invade Great Britain. If they do so they will be driven out by our Navy, our Army and our Air Force. Yet the ordinary men and women of the civilian population will also have their part to play. Hitler's invasions of Poland, Holland and Belgium were greatly helped by the fact that the civilian population was taken by surprise. They did not know what to do when the moment came. *You must not be taken by surprise.* This leaflet tells you what general line you should take. More detailed instructions will be given you when the danger comes nearer. Meanwhile, read these instructions carefully and be prepared to carry them out.

I

When Holland and Belgium were invaded, the civilian population fled from their homes. They crowded on the roads, in cars, in carts, on bicycles and on foot, and so helped the enemy by preventing their own armies from advancing against the invaders. You must not allow that to happen here. Your first rule, therefore, is :—

(1) IF THE GERMANS COME, BY PARACHUTE, AEROPLANE OR SHIP, YOU MUST REMAIN WHERE YOU ARE. THE ORDER IS "STAY PUT".

If the Commander in Chief decides that the place where you live must be evacuated, he will tell you when and how to leave. Until you receive such orders you must remain where you are. If you run away, you will be exposed to far greater danger because you will be machine-gunned from the air as were civilians in Holland and Belgium, and you will also block the roads by which our own armies will advance to turn the Germans out.

II

There is another method which the Germans adopt in their invasion. They make use of the civilian population in order to create confusion and panic. They spread false rumours and issue false instructions. In order to prevent this, you should obey the second rule, which is as follows :—

(2) DO NOT BELIEVE RUMOURS AND DO NOT SPREAD THEM. WHEN YOU RECEIVE AN ORDER, MAKE QUITE SURE THAT IT IS A TRUE ORDER AND NOT A FAKED ORDER. MOST OF YOU KNOW YOUR POLICEMEN AND YOUR A.R.P. WARDENS BY SIGHT, YOU CAN TRUST THEM. IF YOU KEEP YOUR HEADS, YOU CAN ALSO TELL WHETHER A MILITARY OFFICER IS REALLY BRITISH OR ONLY PRETENDING TO BE SO. IF IN DOUBT ASK THE POLICE-MAN OR THE A.R.P. WARDEN. USE YOUR COMMON SENSE.

III

The Army, the Air Force and the Local Defence Volunteers cannot be everywhere at once. The ordinary man and woman must be on the watch. If you see anything suspicious, do not rush round telling your neighbours all about it. Go at once to the nearest policeman, police-station, or military officer and tell them exactly what you saw. Train yourself to notice the exact time and place where you saw anything suspicious, and try to give exact information. Try to check your facts. The sort of report which a military or police officer wants from you is something like this :—

"At 5.30 p.m. to-night I saw twenty cyclists come into Little Squashborough from the direction of Great Mudtown. They carried some sort of automatic rifle or gun. I did not see anything like artillery. They were in grey uniforms."

Be calm, quick and exact. The third rule, therefore, is as follows :—

(3) KEEP WATCH. IF YOU SEE ANYTHING SUSPICIOUS, NOTE IT CAREFULLY AND GO AT ONCE TO THE NEAREST POLICE OFFICER OR STATION, OR TO THE NEAREST MILITARY OFFICER. DO NOT RUSH ABOUT SPREADING VAGUE RUMOURS. GO QUICKLY TO THE NEAREST AUTHORITY AND GIVE HIM THE FACTS.

IV

Remember that if parachutists come down near your home, they will not be feeling at all brave. They will not know where they are, they will have no food, they will not know where their companions are. They will want you to give them food, means of transport and maps. They will want you to tell them where they have landed, where their comrades are, and where our own soldiers are. The fourth rule, therefore, is as follows :—

(4) DO NOT GIVE ANY GERMAN ANYTHING. DO NOT TELL HIM ANYTHING. HIDE YOUR FOOD AND YOUR BICYCLES. HIDE YOUR MAPS. SEE THAT THE ENEMY GETS NO PETROL. IF YOU HAVE A CAR OR MOTOR BICYCLE, PUT IT OUT OF ACTION WHEN NOT IN USE. IT IS NOT ENOUGH TO REMOVE THE IGNITION KEY; YOU MUST MAKE IT USELESS TO ANYONE EXCEPT YOURSELF.

IF YOU ARE A GARAGE PROPRIETOR, YOU MUST WORK OUT A PLAN TO PROTECT YOUR STOCK OF PETROL AND YOUR CUSTOMERS' CARS. REMEMBER THAT TRANSPORT AND PETROL WILL BE THE INVADER'S MAIN DIFFICULTIES. MAKE SURE THAT NO INVADER WILL BE ABLE TO GET HOLD OF YOUR CARS, PETROL, MAPS OR BICYCLES.

V

You may be asked by Army and Air Force officers to help in many ways. For instance, the time may come when you will receive orders to block roads or streets in order to prevent the enemy from advancing. Never block a road unless you are told which one you must block. Then you can help by felling trees, wiring them together or blocking the roads with cars. Here, therefore, is the fifth rule :—

(5) BE READY TO HELP THE MILITARY IN ANY WAY. BUT DO NOT BLOCK ROADS UNTIL ORDERED TO DO SO BY THE MILITARY OR L.D.V. AUTHORITIES.

VI

If you are in charge of a factory, store or other works, organise its defence at once. If you are a worker, make sure that you understand the system of defence that has been organised and know what part you have to play in it. Remember always that parachutists and fifth column men are powerless against any organised resistance. They can only succeed if they can create disorganisation. Make certain that no suspicious strangers enter your premises.

You must know in advance who is to take command, who is to be second in command, and how orders are to be transmitted. This chain of command must be built up and you will probably find that ex-officers or N.C.O.'s, who have been in emergencies before, are the best people to undertake such command. The sixth rule is therefore as follows :—

(6) IN FACTORIES AND SHOPS, ALL MANAGERS AND WORKMEN SHOULD ORGANISE SOME SYSTEM NOW BY WHICH A SUDDEN ATTACK CAN BE RESISTED.

VII

The six rules which you have now read give you a general idea of what to do in the event of invasion. More detailed instructions may, when the time comes, be given you by the Military and Police Authorities and by the Local Defence Volunteers; they will NOT be given over the wireless as that might convey information to the enemy. These instructions must be obeyed at once.

Remember always that the best defence of Great Britain is the courage of her men and women. Here is your seventh rule :—

(7) THINK BEFORE YOU ACT. BUT THINK ALWAYS OF YOUR COUNTRY BEFORE YOU THINK OF YOURSELF.

Did such pamphlets quell fears or foster anxiety?

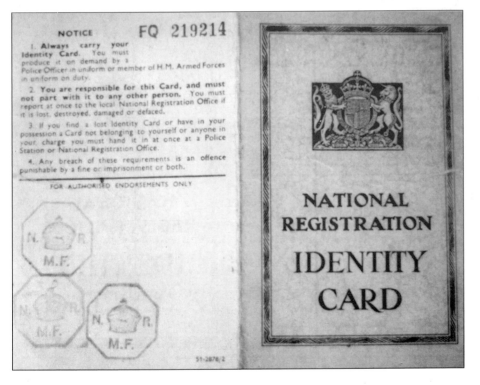

An identity card. This had to be produced on the demand of a police officer or a member of the armed forces.

form of transportation or maps. It concluded, 'Think always of your country before you think of yourself.'

Another leaflet, *Stay Where You Are,* focused on the 'stay put' message, again using the plight of France, Holland and Belgium as a lesson. It pointed out that, 'civilians who try to join in the fight are more likely to get in the way than help. The defeat of an enemy attack is the task of the armed forces which

STAY WHERE YOU ARE

IF this island is invaded by sea or air everyone who is not under orders must stay where he or she is. This is not simply advice : it is an order from the Government, and you must obey it just as soldiers obey their orders. Your order is " Stay Put ", but remember that this does not apply until invasion comes.

Why must I stay put ?

Because in France, Holland and Belgium, the Germans were helped by the people who took flight before them. Great crowds of refugees blocked all roads. The soldiers who could have defended them could not get at the enemy. The enemy used the refugees as a human shield. These refugees were got out on to the roads by rumour and false orders. Do not be caught out in this way. Do not take any notice of any story telling what the enemy has done or where he is. Do not take orders except from the Military, the Police, the Home Guard (L.D.V.) and the A.R.P. authorities or wardens.

What will happen to me if I don't stay put ?

If you do not stay put you will stand a very good chance of being killed. The enemy may machine-gun you from the air in order to increase panic, or you may run into enemy forces which have landed behind you. An official German message was captured in Belgium which ran :

" Watch for civilian refugees on the roads. Harass them as much as possible."

Our soldiers will be hurrying to drive back the invader and will not be able to stop and help you. On the contrary, they will have to turn *you* off the roads so that they can get at the enemy. You will not have reached safety and you will have done just what the enemy wanted you to do.

How shall I prepare to stay put ?

Make ready your air-raid shelter; if you have no shelter prepare one. Advice can be obtained from your local Air Raid Warden or in " Your Home as an Air-raid Shelter ", the Government booklet which tells you how to prepare a shelter in your house that will be strong enough to protect you against stray shots and falling metal. If you can have a trench ready in your garden or field, so much the better, especially if you live where there is likely to be danger from shell-fire.

How can I help ?

You can help by setting a good example to others. Civilians who try to join in the fight are more likely to get in the way than to help. The defeat of an enemy attack is the task of the armed forces which include the Home Guard, so if you wish to fight enrol in the Home Guard. If there is no vacancy for you at the moment register your name for enrolment and you will be called upon as soon as the Army is ready to employ you. For those who cannot join there are many ways in which the Military and Home Guard may need your help in their preparations. Find out what you can do to help in any local defence work that is going on, and be ready to turn your hand to anything if asked by the Military or Home Guard to do so.

If you are responsible for the safety of a factory or some other important building, get in touch with the nearest military authority. You will then be told how your defence should fit in with the military organisation and plans.

What shall I do if the Invader comes my way ?

If fighting by organised forces is going on in your district and you have no special duties elsewhere, go to your shelter and stay there till the battle is past. Do not attempt to join in the fight. Behave as if an air-raid were going on. The enemy will seldom turn aside to attack separate houses.

But if small parties are going about threatening persons and property in an area not under enemy control and come your way, you have the right of every man and woman to do what you can to protect yourself, your family and your home.

Stay put.

It's easy to say. When the time comes it may be hard to do. But you have got to do it; and in doing it you will be fighting Britain's battle as bravely as a soldier.

---

include the Home Guard, so if you wish to fight enrol in the Home Guard.' So if an invasion did take place, what were civilians to do?

'If fighting by organised forces is going on in your district ... go to your shelter and stay there till the battle is past. Do not attempt to join in the fight. Behave as if an air raid were going on.'

Beating the INVADER, printed in May 1941, included a message from the Prime Minister and fourteen questions and answers. As well as repeating the advice about retreating to a shelter in the event of an invasion, it advised against laying in extra food and gave tips on disabling vehicles. It said who would give orders and advice and explained that if the church bells – which had been silenced at the outbreak of war – were to ring, this was to warn 'the local garrison that troops have been seen landing from the air in the neighbourhood of the church in question.' This would not lead to a general ringing of the church bells.

Question 3 asked 'Will certain roads and railways be reserved for the use of the Military, even in areas far from the scene of action?' The answer to this was, 'Yes, certain roads will have to be reserved for important troop movements; but such reservations should only be temporary.' In fact, a letter to Cornwall County Council Highways Department had advised that The Emergency Powers (Defence) Traffic on Highways Order 1940, made by the Minister of

Issued by the Ministry of Information in co-operation with the War Office and the Ministry of Home Security

Beating the INVADER

A MESSAGE FROM THE PRIME MINISTER

IF invasion comes, everyone—young or old, men and women—will be eager to play their part worthily. By far the greater part of the country will not be immediately involved. Even along our coasts, the greater part will remain unaffected. But where the enemy lands, or tries to land, there will be most violent fighting. Not only will there be the battles when the enemy tries to come ashore, but afterwards there will fall upon his lodgments very heavy British counter-attacks, and all the time the lodgments will be under the heaviest attack by British bombers. The fewer civilians or non-combatants in these areas, the better—apart from essential workers who must remain. So if you are advised by the authorities to leave the place where you live, it is your duty to go elsewhere when you are told to leave. When the attack begins, it will be too late to go ; and, unless you receive definite instructions to move, your duty then will be to stay where you are. You will have to get into the safest place you can find, and stay there until the battle is over. For all of you then the order and the duty will be: " STAND FIRM ".

This also applies to people inland if any considerable number of parachutists or air-borne troops are landed in their neighbourhood. Above all, they must not cumber the roads. Like their fellow-countrymen on the coasts, they must " STAND FIRM ". The Home Guard, supported by strong mobile columns wherever the enemy's numbers require it, will immediately come to grips with the invaders, and there is little doubt will soon destroy them.

Throughout the rest of the country where there is no fighting going on and no close cannon fire or rifle fire can be heard, everyone will govern his conduct by the second great order and duty, namely, " CARRY ON ". It may easily be some weeks before the invader has been totally destroyed, that is to say, killed or captured to the last man who has landed on our shores. Meanwhile, all work must be continued to the utmost, and no time lost.

The following notes have been prepared to tell everyone in rather more detail what to do, and they should be carefully studied. Each man and woman should think out a clear plan of personal action in accordance with the general scheme.

Winston S. Churchill

STAND FIRM

1. What do I do if fighting breaks out in my neighbourhood?

Keep indoors or in your shelter until the battle is over. If you can have a trench ready in your garden or field, so much the better. You may want to use it for protection if your house is damaged. But if you are at work, or if you have special orders, carry on as long as possible and only take cover when danger approaches. If you are on your way to work, finish your journey if you can.

If you see an enemy tank, or a few enemy soldiers, do not assume that the enemy are in control of the area. What you have seen may be a party sent on in advance, or stragglers from the main body who can easily be rounded up.

CARRY ON

2. What do I do in areas which are some way from the fighting?

Stay in your district and carry on. Go to work whether in shop, field, factory or office. Do your shopping, send your children to school until you are told not to. Do not try to go and live somewhere else. Do not use the roads for any unnecessary journey ; they must be left free for troop movements even a long way from the district where actual fighting is taking place.

3. Will certain roads and railways be reserved for the use of the Military, even in areas far from the scene of action?

Yes, certain roads will have to be reserved for important troop movements ; but such reservations should be only temporary. As far as possible, bus companies and railways will try to maintain essential public services, though it may be necessary to cut these down. Bicyclists and pedestrians may use the roads for journeys to work, unless instructed not to do so.

ADVICE AND ORDERS

4. Whom shall I ask for advice?
The police and A.R.P. wardens.

5. From whom shall I take orders?
In most cases from the police and A.R.P. wardens. But there may be times when you will have to take orders from the military and the Home Guard in uniform.

6. Is there any means by which I can tell that an order is a true order and not faked?
You will generally know your policeman and your A.R.P. wardens by sight, and can trust them. With a bit of common sense you can tell if a soldier is really British or only pretending to be so. If in doubt ask a policeman, or ask a soldier whom you know personally.

INSTRUCTIONS

7. What does it mean when the church bells are rung?
It is a warning to the local garrison that troops have been seen landing from the air in the neighbourhood of the church in question. Church bells will *not* be rung all over the country as a general warning that invasion has taken place. The ringing of church bells in one place will not be taken up in neighbouring churches.

8. Will instructions be given over the wireless?
Yes ; so far as possible. But remember that the enemy can overhear any wireless message, so that the wireless cannot be used for instructions which might give him valuable information.

9. In what other ways will instructions be given?
Through the Press ; by loudspeaker vans ; and perhaps by leaflets and posters. But remember that genuine Government leaflets will be given to you only by the policeman, your A.R.P. warden or your postman ; while genuine posters and instructions will be put up only on Ministry of Information notice boards and official sites, such as police stations, post offices, A.R.P. posts, town halls and schools.

FOOD

10. Should I try to lay in extra food?
No. If you have already laid in a stock of food, keep it for a real emergency ; but do not add to it. The Government has made arrangements for food supplies.

NEWS

11. Will normal news services continue?
Yes. Careful plans have been made to enable newspapers and wireless broadcasts to carry on, and in case of need there are emergency measures which will bring you the news. But if there should be some temporary breakdown in news supply, it is very important that you should not listen to rumours nor pass them on. Wait till real news comes through again. Do not use the telephones or send telegrams if you can possibly avoid it.

MOTOR-CARS

12. Should I put my car, lorry or motor-bicycle out of action?
Yes, when you are told to do so by the police, A.R.P. wardens or military ; or when it is obvious that there is an immediate risk of its being seized by the enemy—then disable and hide your bicycle and destroy your maps.

13. How should it be put out of action?
Remove distributor head and leads and either empty the tank or remove the carburettor. If you don't know how to do this, find out now from your nearest garage. In the case of diesel engines remove the injection pump and connection. The parts removed must be hidden well away from the vehicle.

THE ENEMY

14. Should I defend myself against the enemy?
The enemy is not likely to turn aside to attack separate houses. If small parties are going about threatening persons and property in an area not under enemy control and come your way, you have the right of every man and woman to do what you can to protect yourself, your family and your home.

GIVE ALL THE HELP YOU CAN TO OUR TROOPS

Do not tell the enemy anything

Do not give him anything

Do not help him in any way

(55001) Wt. 46361/P1009 14,650,000 (2 kds.) 5/41 Hw. G.51

Transport on 1 July 1940, provided for prohibiting or regulating the use of vehicles or highways 'for the purpose of meeting or hindering any actual or apprehended attack by an enemy…'[8]

In any event, travel was discouraged with messages like 'Is Your Journey Really Necessary?' and when it was, venturing out could be both difficult and dangerous. In 1939 The Home Office Air Raid Precautions Department issued a booklet, *Memorandum on Aids to the Movement of Traffic to be Installed in Roads*

First Aid practice at Grampound. It is interesting that they have taken the trouble to label the helmets with FAP, presumably to reassure onlookers that it was only a practice.

'Is Your Journey Really Necessary?'

A headlamp shroud fitted to a Jeep.

and Streets in the Absence of Street Lighting. This provided guidance for local authorities on the screening of illuminated bollards and the use of traffic signal masks and mandatory signs. It also provided details of where white paint should be applied. [9]

So that they could not be spotted from the sky, car headlights had to be partly obscured by covers with hoods or slits in them. White paint also had to be applied to cars' running boards to make them more visible, as well as the bumpers, although some motorists attached a piece of white-painted wood to them rather than deface their vehicles.

Accident rates soared. It was recognised in the local newspaper that, 'Normal road risks are many times greater in the black-out. Ordinary precaution (sic) should therefore be greatly increased. In a sentence: Keep your wits about you and "Look out in the Black-out."' [10] In a separate statement on the next page it warned that nearly 1200 people had been killed in December alone. In fact, more people died on British roads between August and December 1940 than those killed on active service. [11] In an attempt to halt the carnage a 20 mph speed limit in built-up areas was introduced. However drivers found it difficult to abide by this rule when the car's dashboard could not be illuminated!

The black-out also led to some curious road traffic offences being committed. In March 1940 a Fowey man was fined 5/- for parking his car on the wrong side of the road. He said he had forgotten the new law. [12] Meanwhile other motorists were caught out by other changes of legislation:

> West Powder Bench at Truro on Thursday dealt with the first charges which have been brought before them under the law requiring motorists to render their cars immobile. [13]

In another incident black-out legislation led to people being caught whilst carrying out nefarious nocturnal activities; lamping rabbits. Four men were fined a total of £7 at Truro for poaching 61 rabbits from a farm at Blackwater, and were also charged with showing an unscreened light! [14]

In September 1944, as the threat of invasion diminished, black-out regulations were lifted to allow lights on buses, trains and at railway stations. This relaxation was known as 'half lighting'.

As well as the hazards presented by black-out regulations, those motorists able to venture out also had to contend with road barriers which were set up on many highways. These came in various forms (see diagram on page 45).

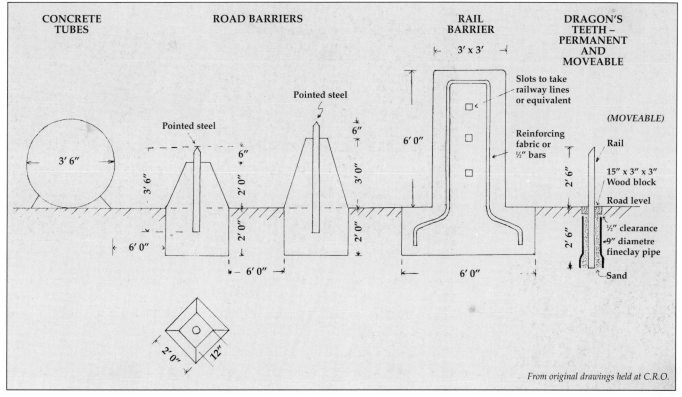

| CONCRETE TUBES | ROAD BARRIERS | RAIL BARRIER | DRAGON'S TEETH – PERMANENT AND MOVEABLE |

From original drawings held at C.R.O.

Various types of road barriers were designed and installed on Cornwall's highways.

Concrete tubes could be arranged horizontally or vertically and used in conjunction with steel spikes or dragon's teeth to restrict the road width. As a supposed warning the white lines were terminated a hundred feet before a road block, 'to indicate to the motorist that he will have to exercise special care.' [15] (It was assumed that any motorist would be male, although the war was to give many women their first taste of driving.)

No doubt there were a number of accidents, for a more pragmatic approach was later taken, with solid white lines added to roadblocks on 'Essential Routes and Class 1 Roads', plus hooded lamps showing a red light. [16]

Some roads also had 'aeroplane traps' using posts and wires or 'pyramids' to prevent them being used as landing strips. These were to be maintained by the Highways authority. [17] Pillboxes were also constructed next to some routes.

Various types of anti-tank obstacles were also developed. These came in various shapes and sizes, including 'Pimples' to create small obstacles; Buoys – for use on hard roads only – which were reinforced concrete truncated cones with spherical bases, spaced irregularly at six-foot centres in five rows; and Cylinders. The latter, spaced in a similar manner, were interspersed with bricks, kerbstones, or any convenient rubble, to prevent them rolling. Cast steel eyes in the bottom of the cylinders enabled steel wires of a half-inch diameter to link them together so it would be more difficult for tanks to sweep them aside. [18]

Road signs and place names were removed to foil Fifth Columnists or an invasion party, but in the event this probably did more to hinder the local population. The same thing had happened in the Channel Islands – where there is still a dearth of road signs today – but the enemy still seemed to have remarkable intelligence and were not inconvenienced.

In 1940 railings and metal fences were removed from parks and private gardens to provide the raw materials for industry. Even the railings round the daymark on Gribbin Head near Fowey were removed, and would not be

WAIT

YOU CAN SEE THE CAR –WHEN THE DRIVER CAN'T SEE YOU!

4 SIMPLE RULES *for getting home safely in the black-out*

1 When you first come out into the black-out, stand still for a minute to get your eyes used to the darkness.

2 Look *both* ways before stepping off the pavement. Make *sure* there's nothing coming.

3 Where there are traffic lights, always cross by them. It is worth going out of your way to do this.

4 Throw the light of your torch down on to the ground.

LOOK OUT IN THE BLACK-OUT!

Travelling at night could be difficult and dangerous. Advice such as this tried to stem the mounting casualty figures.

A tank trap now forms an ideal signpost at Porthpean near St Austell (above).

Members of Stithians Home Guard manning a barricade. Left to right, back: R. Dunstan, J. Pascoe, E. Perry, Sgt. Moore; front: W. Burley, C. Spargo. The substantial crossbar supported on a cross frame was no doubt just as effective as the methods outlined by the local authorities (above right).

A deliberately defaced sign. It should read 'St Austell School Board Charlestown School'. The ceilings of a classroom at the school and cloakroom collapsed when a bomb landed in a nearby field in 5 July 1940 after a He-111 attempted to bomb a column of troops (right).

The daymark on The Gribbin near Fowey. The railings, removed during the war, are finally being replaced in October 2001 (below).

Behind the railings on the left-hand side once stood a small stone hut use by the local Home Guard during their nightly patrols (below right).

replaced until the autumn of 2001. A 'Saucepans for Spitfires' campaign was launched by the Minister of Aircraft Production, Lord Beaverbrook. Although it was not realised at the time, this was merely a propaganda exercise, the metal being of too poor a quality to be of any use. However, this was followed by demands for rags, bottles, waste paper, as well as other commodities.

Advertisements in local newspapers stated:

SALVAGE
Save all your Waste for Weapons
of War
If you do all you can you
cannot do more. [19]

Promoting war savings.
PUBLIC RECORD OFFICE

More successful were the campaigns such as War Weapons Week, when firms and individuals were encouraged to invest in Savings Bonds, National War Bonds, Defence Bonds, etc. As pointed out in the *Royal Cornwall Gazette*, 'The War Weapons Week differs from the Spitfire Fund in that gifts of money are not being appealed for, but … saving and lending money to the country. [20]

Local campaigns were very successful and often broke their targets. St Austell's War Weapons Week in March 1941 raised £103 000, £3000 more than the target, [21] while the following week Truro City and Rural District passed its target of £100 000 by over £12 000. [22] West Cornwall's War Weapons Week exceeded their target four-fold, raising £460 096; 'though the district was keenly disappointed at failing to pass the record of £483 518 set by Camborne-Redruth.' [23]

This campaign was followed by Warship Week which was also conducted through the sale of bonds. St Austell's Warship Week 'to launch a large Minesweeper and a Trawler Minesweeper,' [24] opened with a parade. The target of Fowey's Warship Week was £14 000, the cost of a harbour defence craft. In the event, the town raised £27 226; 'equal to nearly £7 per head of the population of the area.' [25] Meanwhile, in the first day of Penzance and District's Warship Week, £38 221 was raised. [26]

Also very successful was the Spitfire Fund. This appealed to the residents of towns to collect £5000 for a Spitfire or even a part of an aeroplane, as illustrated by this newspaper article:

This fine plaque was produced in recognition of Fowey's contribution towards Salute the Soldier Week.

Mr John Delbridge, who, as Mayor of Truro, organised a County Spitfire Fund, sent a cheque for £5500 to Lord Beaverbrook… The cheque was accompanied by a request that the machine to be provided and equipped out of the fund shall be named 'Cornwall'. [27]

This wish was duly granted. The name was awarded to a Spitfire Mk.IIB, serial number P8669. It was issued to 303 Squadron on 1 July 1941. [28]

Other districts of Cornwall raised enough money to purchase 'their own' Spitfires. Camborne and Redruth also furnished the airforce with a Mk.IIB, serial number P8671. It was first flown by 118 Squadron from 30 June 1941, then by 132 Squadron from 14 October until 10 April 1942. Then it was used for training by 10 OTU (Operational Training Unit), but twelve months later, following an engine failure, it crash-landed on Goswick Sands, near Holy Island in Northumberland. When the tide came in the wreckage was washed out to sea.

Similar fates befell the St Ives and Scillonian Spitfires. The St Ives aircraft, serial number BL709, was issued to 340 Squadron on 1 March 1942, but only managed to complete about seventy-five hours flying time before it was seriously damaged in a flying accident on 14 May 1943, leading to it being struck off charge the following month. 'Scillonia', a Mk.I, serial number X4623, was used by 610 Squadron from 17 October 1940. It was later transferred to 602 Squadron who used it until the following November. After being withdrawn from operational flying, it was flown by student crews of 61 and 51 OTUs. Although damaged in a flying accident in March 1943, it was repaired and continued to be used for training until the final year of the war. [29] Meanwhile, St Austell and District's Spitfire, used for photographic reconnaissance, was shot down (See Chapter 5).

There was a constant need to fund and build more planes. As well as reports in the local papers extolling the fund-raising of various towns, and frequent advertisements encouraging the purchase of various types of war bonds, a crashed Messerschmitt Bf 109E-1 was sent round the county as a way of capturing interest, as well as encouraging people to give, so that even more might meet a similar fate.

Launceston Wings for Victory Parade, 12 June 1943. Taking the salute in the Square.
GEORGE ELLIS COLLECTION

British prisoners of war were not forgotten in Cornwall. PoW Weeks were held which raised money through traditional events such as bring-and-buy stalls, jumble sales, dances etc. Cornwall's Prisoners of War Parcels Fund supported the efforts of the Red Cross in providing food parcels. In 1943, the Parish of St Dennis raised £17 16s 9d. The cost of each parcel was 10/- and the Red Cross aimed to send one per prisoner each week. These usually contained tins and packets of foodstuff, cigarettes and soap, and occasionally knitted garments or seeds for growing common vegetables in their camps. The parcels provided a welcome supplement to what was provided by their captors, as well as being a great morale booster. In May 1943 the St Austell area had 17 PoWs in enemy camps. [30]

With the war intruding into almost every aspect of people's lives, it became more and more difficult to find escape. One popular pastime was the cinema, to see films such as *The Stars Look Down,* co-starring Michael Redgrave, Margaret Lockwood and Emlyn Williams, billed as 'The Greatest Film of them all!' It also included 'Britain's finest newsreel – The Paramount News', [31] which would have provided censored and propagandist war-time news. More light-hearted yet poignant entertainment was Charlie Chaplin's *The Great Dictato*r, shown at the Odeon, St Austell in March 1941 and the Regent Theatre, Truro, the following month.

Bodmin's Salute the Soldier Week, 29 April 1943, showing the DCLI Band going up Fore Street.

GEORGE ELLIS COLLECTION

Another source of news and entertainment was the wireless, a universal medium for much of the free world. Television, still in its infancy, was not available, since the BBC had stopped broadcasting at the start of the war, it being feared that enemy planes would be able to pick up the signals and use them to home in on their targets. (German television continued to broadcast, because of its value as a propaganda tool.)

Vital links with the outside world were also maintained in a covert manner. In the valley above Porthcurno Cove a secret communication centre was con-

A sentry outside 'The Tunnel' underground telegraph station, Porthcurno, 1941. This provides an interesting comparison with the German uniforms on p.40.

structed. Following the fall of France, an underground telegraph station was built into the east side of the hill in order to protect a cable and radio network of over 355 000 miles. This was a vital system that maintained communications with the rest of the British empire for, of the two, cables were more secure than radio communications, which could be intercepted.

The tunnels were begun in June 1940, the contract being awarded to Edmund Nuttall & Co. At the height of construction 225 men worked on the site, completing the project in May 1941. Blast-proof doors a foot thick were installed in the entrance tunnel and fitted with gas-proof rubber seals. As an added precaution a circle of gas-sensitive paint was applied to each door to warn of attacks. The entrance led into a large instrument room which, apart from the absence of windows, belied the fact that it was subterranean. 'The Tunnel' underground telegraph station also comprised a workshop and escape stairs of 112 steps linking it with the hill above. Cut through solid granite, dripping with water, the escape route was also fitted with blast-proof doors and bullet deflectors.

The importance of the station was reflected in the fact that a police guard was posted at the entrance. There were 11 men, classed as Police Reserves, working in three eight-hour watches, who were paid wages, unlike Special Constables. [32] In May, following an inspection, the Chief Camouflage Officer of The Ministry of Home Security advised that any buildings that were 'white or conspicuously light in colour should be painted a dark grey', and even enclosed a colour card, though they considered that no other action needed to be taken. [33] In July 1940, as the threat of invasion increased, 200 soldiers arrived and a survey was undertaken for the mounting of four anti-aircraft artillery

guns. [34] In addition, three pillboxes were constructed to defend Porthcurno Cove, one on the headland to the east, with two others close together overlooking the beach on the western side.

An FW3/27 Pillbox overlooking Porthcurno Cove

CHAPTER 3 – REFERENCES

(PC = Personal Communication)

[1] Winston Churchill in *Beating the INVADER* leaflet, May 1941.

[2] *Royal Cornwall Gazette*, 20 March 1940.

[3] *What to do about Gas* (55189), April 1941.

[4] Ibid.

[5] Ibid.

[6] Plans for this building, as well as those for gas-proof shutters, shelving for GS respirators, steel helmet hangars, etc., are held at the Cornwall Record Office, Truro.

[7] County ARP Records, p. 18, Cornwall Record Office, Truro.

[8] Cornwall Record Office, Truro.

[9] Ibid.

[10] *Royal Cornwall Gazette*, 14 February 1940, p. 2.

[11] *The British Motorist* (1987), Lord Montagu of Beaulieu, p. 101.

[12] *Royal Cornwall Gazette*, 20 March 1940, p. 5.

[13] *Royal Cornwall Gazette*, 21 August 1940, p. 4.

[14] *Royal Cornwall Gazette*, 24 April 1940, p. 3.

[15] Letter from Cornwall County Council Roads and Bridges Department to Divisional & Assistant Divisional Surveyors, 5 July 1940 (Cornwall Record Office, Truro).

[16] Letter from Ministry of Transport Road Department (Southern Division) Exeter, to Cornwall County Council, 17 October 1940 (Cornwall Record Office, Truro).

[17] Letter from Cornwall County Council Highways Department, 15 January 1941 (Cornwall Record Office, Truro).

[18] Based on a letter from the County Surveyor to DCRE Cornwall, 2 December 1940 (Cornwall Record Office, Truro).

[19] *West Briton* 17, November 1941, p. 4.

[20] *Royal Cornwall Gazette*, 5 March 1941, p. 3.

[21] *Royal Cornwall Gazette*, 12 March 1941, p. 2.

[22] *Royal Cornwall Gazette*, 19 March 1941, p. 2.

[23] *Royal Cornwall Gazette*, 7 May 1941, p. 4.

[24] *Royal Cornwall Gazette*, 26 November 1941, p. 3.

[25] Ibid.

[26] Ibid.

[27] *Royal Cornwall Gazette*, 13 November 1940, p. 4.

The instrument room in 'The Tunnel' underground telegraph station during the 1940s (opposite).

COURTESY OF THE MUSEUM OF
SUBMARINE TELEGRAPHY, PORTHCURNO

[28] PC: Mr F. Harper.

[29] Ibid.

[30] Letter from Clerk of Council to British Red Cross Society, 10 May 1943 (Cornwall Record Office, Truro).

[31] *Royal Cornwall Gazette*, 24 April 1940, p. 6.

[32] In a secret letter to Cable & Wireless Ltd, 16 March 1940.

[33] Letter to Cable & Wireless Ltd, 1 May 1940.

[34] In a telegram to Cable & Wireless Ltd, 7 July 1940.

4

WAR WORK

The whole of the warring nations are engaged, not only soldiers, but the entire population; men, women and children. The fronts are everywhere. The trenches are dug in towns and streets. Every village is fortified. Every road is barred. The front lines run through the factories. The workmen are soldiers with different weapons, but with the same courage.

CHURCHILL [1]

By the outbreak of the Second World War Cornwall's traditional industries, farming, fishing and mining, had been augmented by the china-clay industry in mid-Cornwall, as well as engineering and a burgeoning tourist industry. The latter had been born with the arrival of the Great Western Railway which put the West Country within reach of the inhabitants of the cities. Tourism had been promoted by the Cornish Riviera service, and hotels had been developed to cater for the visitors to seaside towns like Newquay, Falmouth and St Ives. A colourful poster campaign compared Cornwall with the French Riviera, only the Duchy had the advantage of being more accessible and more affordable.

Now, at a time of war, many of the hotels had been requisitioned by the forces, or were used as hospitals or HQs (See Chapter 8). An advertisement issued by the National Savings Committee, London, stated; 'We must put aside all thought of going away for holidays until this war is over and victory is won.' [2] Furthermore, holiday and pleasure trips to certain areas were prohibited and parents visiting evacuated children had to register with their local authorities who would provide them with a monthly voucher. [3]

Food supplies, previously taken for granted when they arrived by sea from the Empire, were now restricted, and farming took on a new imperative. The situation was compounded with the fall of Denmark, Holland, Belgium, Luxembourg and France, the suppliers of over 1 750 000 tons of our foodstuffs. These countries accounted for over half our bacon and ham, eggs, condensed milk and milk powder and 30 per cent of our butter. [4] Land that had lain idle was tilled and householders were urged to give up their borders and flower beds in a bid to 'Dig for Victory'.

At the outbreak of war each of the 15 Food Executive Officers, who were each responsible for a division of the country as set out by the Food (Defence Plans) Department, received a coded telegram to begin work. They set up Food Executive Offices and appointed a Local Food Control Committee. Meanwhile the Cultivation of Lands Order 1939 called for the setting up of War Agricultural Committees in each county. They were responsible for increasing food production. To aid this process farmers were offered £2 per acre that was ploughed, so long as it had been in grass for seven years – and provided it was done by the end of 1939. The deadline was later extended to 30 April 1940.

Two posters from the 'Dig For Victory' campaign.

On 13 March 1940 a quarter-page advertisement in the *Royal Cornwall Gazette* stated:

Farmers! Plough now by day and night. Play your part in the fight for right.' [5]

This must have been hazardous in black-out conditions. The advertisement also contained a box with the message:

The Prime Minister, speaking on February 20th: The Minister of Agriculture made a pronouncement last December, when he said, 'If the increase in home production that we want is to be obtained, then the prices must be such as would give a reasonable return to the farmer and enable the farmer to pay a fair wage to the worker.' I want to say again that the War Cabinet endorse that declaration by the Minister of Agriculture. [6]

This message was repeated in sebsequent advertisements, along with exhultations like:

Plough the Fields
Increase Their Yields
Plough up your grassland.

Make every field give a greater yield. You cannot grow guns and planes; but you can grow more food and more root and fodder crops, so releasing ships to carry guns and planes. Make no mistake – ploughing is the key to victory – and the key is in your hands. Plough Now! [7]

By that spring nearly 2 million acres had been tilled. [8]

In June the Minister of Food's focus of attention had changed from food production to consumption. Now he urged:

We should eat more Potatoes. They give energy and protection against illness. They are home-grown. More Potatoes mean less bread and fewer ships to bring wheat from overseas. Above all avoid waste and so save shipping. [9]

In November 1940 the Government announced that British summertime was to continue through the winter months. Then in May 1941 'double summertime' was introduced, again with the intention of increasing production, but also lengthening the working day of agricultural workers.

Meanwhile war was not just being waged on the Germans. There was an invidious enemy much closer to home, according to a column in the newspaper in December:

It's Doing Hitler's Work

Kill that Rat!

From wallowing in unmentionable filth, these pests invade our larders, our food shops, our warehouses, gnawing and pawing and wasting food. Kill them now! [10]

And so it went on…

Fertilisers were no longer available, so beach sand was used. During the construction of Davidstow airfield the lorries would return via Harlyn Bay to collect sand for distribution to farms.

To avoid inflation, and to provide a system that was fair to everybody, the Government introduced rationing from 8 January 1940. There was no surprise in this; it had been used at the end of the First World War, and ration books had been printed as early as 1938 following the Munich crisis. These were actually issued in October 1939 and the public had until 23 November to register at a shop where they intended to buy their provisions. Initially each person was restricted to 4 ounces of bacon or ham, 4 ounces of butter and 12 ounces of sugar a week. The amounts and type of food would vary depending on supply and demand, and for many, despite their complaints, it led to a more healthy diet.

In rural Cornwall the rationed food could be augmented by what could be produced at home, either by growing fruit and vegetables, or by keeping a pig, chickens or geese in the back garden, even if animal feed itself was rationed!

There were local concerns about what was being rationed. On 21 February 1940, a Mr J.R. Rathbone of Bodmin was reported to have put a written question to the Minister of Food asking whether Cornish pasties would be included under the heading of meat pies for exemption from rationing restrictions. Mr W.S. Morrison replied giving the assurance asked for, much to the relief no doubt of many in the county. [11]

The 'Grow More Food' campaign changed in 1940 after a London evening paper coined the more snappy phrase, 'Dig for Victory'. In February 1941 the first 'Dig for Victory' leaflets appeared. Each of the 25 different versions concentrated on different ways of improving cultivation.

To make up for the shortfall in the agricultural labour force, in May 1939 the Women's Land Army was re-established. Again, it had first come into exis-

Yet more advice. Ration books became a part of everyday life (left). A series of guides was published by the Ministry of Food to help housewives (right).

tence during the First World War. Before they took up work they were provided with a month's training at a farm institute or college. In Cornwall 'Bosahan' House on the Helford River, the home of Lord and Lady Seaton, was used as a training centre. The recruits would then be sent to a farm where their services were required; otherwise they might work in large private gardens, as long as a proportion of their work was for food production. The WLA would eventually have 90 000 members. [12]

Agricultural labour was also provided by the inmates of prisoner-of-war camps. There were several camps in Cornwall: Pennygillam and Scarnecross

One of the many aids to gardening issued by the Ministry of Agriculture as part of the Dig For Victory campaign (left).

Promoting the Women's Land Army (below left). *No longer just the work of men* (below).

Land Girls at Sargin Sawmills, 6 July 1945, illustrates the diversity of work that was undertaken by them.

GEORGE ELLIS COLLECTION

Camps near Launceston; Consols Mine Camp at Lanescot near Par; Whitecross Halt Camp near St Columb Major; Bowithick on Bodmin Moor; Bake at Trerulefoot and another near Mylor Bridge.

Whitecross Halt Camp was built next to the railway track and covered an area of approximately 12 acres. The site was laid out in ranks of white concrete huts and was dominated by a tall water tower. Around a thousand prisoners were held there. Originally these were Italians, but later most of them were moved out and it held German PoWs. The Italians built their own elaborately decorated church with a beautiful altar, but the latter was later destroyed by the German PoWs.

Besides the church, the inmates were allowed to level ground and construct a football pitch. The prisoners were organised into five teams and ran their own league. According to an Italian PoW, they were well treated and given the same food as the local people. Peirone Ferruccio, an inmate from 1943–1946, acted as an English/Italian/German interpreter. He recalls, 'I assure you that during the war I appreciated the behaviour of English military personal (sic) and of your people'. [13]

Whitecross was an 'open' prison and as such had no formal gateway. Escapes do not seem to have been a problem, as they were so well treated. For many, conditions were better than at home and they didn't want to return to have to rejoin the war. In fact, the German medical officer is said to have made regular trips on the train to Newquay to see his girlfriend – on condition that he returned by the 18:00 hr curfew. At the end of the war some Italians chose to stay in Britain and sent for their families to join them here.

The prisoners worked on local farms and, as well as being housed and fed, were also paid a small wage. An idiosyncrasy of German farming methods that caught the attention of the locals was their practice of tying the horses' reins behind their backs and steering with their bodies rather than their hands.

Today the site has been turned into a holiday park. A few of the huts remain, though the exteriors have been plastered and pebbledashed. The water tower still stands and is used as a workshop. Unfortunately, the church was demolished some time ago to make way for a new building. The football field, indistinguishable from the rest of the camp, provides a level pitch for car-avans. Apart from the former Italian and German PoWs, some of whom have made return visits, few of the holidaymakers today can be aware of the park's unusual past!

Changes were also occurring in Cornwall's other indigenous industries. During the 1860s tin had become Cornwall's most important metalliferous mineral. Since reaching a peak in 1856, copper extraction had dramatically declined as viable deposits became exhausted. The depression of 1930 led to a disastrous slump in the price of tin, when it reached its lowest price since the

Whitecross Halt PoW Camp watertower, now part of Summer Lodge Holiday Park (above).

Bars over the window of a solitary confinement hut at Whitecross Halt Camp (above right).

Some of the huts used by the inmates now provide holiday accomodation (right).

turn of the century. There was a corresponding drop in production, from 3271 tons of metal in 1929 to 598 tons in 1931. Subsequently both production and the price obtained per ton had steadily risen, so that by the outbreak of war the annual production was back to approximately 2000 tons. [14]

With the war came a fresh impetus for mining. After the Japanese had overrun the Far East, imports of two important metals, tin and tungsten, had dried up. There was a fresh need to become self-sufficient and the Cornish mines were an obvious source. This view was expounded at the time by one of the leading authorities on Cornish mining, Jack Trounson, who was then an assistant surveyor at South Crofty Mine, as well as a member of 4th Platoon D Company (Redruth) Home Guard. He wrote of:

> ...the imperative need to obtain from Cornwall the maximum amount of tin, tungsten, arsenic, and other vital metals that can be produced ... within a limited period. [15]

Bemoaning the decline in Cornish mining during the previous twenty years Trounson continued:

> ...it is quite obvious that any increase that can be achieved in time to assist the winning of the war can only amount to a very small percentage of the actual demand. [16]

He saw that there were several obstacles to increasing production: a shortage of skilled labour; a lack of a price structure; problems in obtaining machinery; as well as taxation and capital restrictions. He considered production costs were so high and the prices the mines were receiving for the ore was so low, that mining companies were unable to match the wages which could be earned in munitions factories. The loss of skilled men was compounded by the number of men who had been called up. When the original Schedule of Reserved Occupations had been drawn up in November 1938 miners under the age of twenty-three had not been reserved. This was later amended, but by then the harm had been done. He was also amazed to see, '...that Cornish miners were still being encouraged to travel to African copper mines,' [17] despite the shortage of skilled labour in Cornwall.

Formal control of the mines was now with the Non-ferrous Metals Control Division, part of the Ministry of Supply. When the London Metal Exchange closed in December 1941 they became the sole UK buyer and seller of tin, thereby freezing prices.

Cornwall's most important mines at the time were Geevor, South Crofty and East Pool and Agar. Geevor remained buoyant, East Pool and Agar was struggling, but the most productive tin mine was South Crofty. However, discontent with pay and conditions, and a dispute between the Transport & General Workers Union and the management, led to a strike there in January 1939. Animosity turned to violence between strikers and blacklegs. It was not until August, with growing international tension distracting the protagonists, that the dispute ended.

By now many of Cornwall's famous mines had closed as a result of the First World War, the slump of 1920 and during the Depression. These included Botallack in 1914; Garlidna in 1917; Wheal Grenville in 1920; Levant in 1930 and Porkellis Mine in Wendron in 1938. The following examples show the problems facing Cornish mines at the time. Wheal Kitty in St Agnes, which had closed in 1930, had been taken over by a new company in 1937, Polberro Tin, Ltd. They soon had financial difficulties resulting from trying to develop the mine, yet an appeal to the Government failed to secure the necessary finance to reach the rich lodes which were known to be there. The venture ended in March 1941. The Government's view at the time was that any investment and exploration had to be short-term, i.e. within twelve months. In 1942 the Ministry of Supply was not prepared to agree to a new tunnel being sunk at East Pool and Agar Mine, despite the urgent need for tin and tungsten, two important alloying elements. However, direct Government assistance allowed mining there to continue, though in reality the low grade of ore was uneconomic. This lack of investment led to the mine's closure in 1947. Although the Government did encourage prospecting between 1942 and 1944 under the guidance of the Cornish Tin Advisory Committee, there was little chance of finding much of significance that had not been surveyed in previous centuries. Even mines such as Castle-an-Dinas, which had expanded to satisfy the need for wolfram, struggled as their actual output continued to fluctuate. [18]

Castle-an-Dinas Wolfram Mine, 1945.

Those miners who remained saw their wages increase – by as much as 60 per cent between 1937 and 1943. [19] The miners saw changes too; more modern machinery was introduced and some new levels opened. There were also new faces, such as the 'Bevan boys' who were sent to the mines rather than to join the army.

Similar problems beset the china-clay industry. Even before the war the china-clay companies of mid-Cornwall were having a difficult time. During the 1930s several small companies merged with English Clays Lovering Pochin & Co. Ltd (ECLP) of St Austell, or came under the newly formed Goonvean & Rostowrack China-Clay Company Ltd. Also, several paper companies had realised that it was more economic to buy their own pits. So, 'the decade was one of international unrest and already by 1938, when Europe stood on the brink of war, exports of clay had fallen by about 20 per cent.' [20]

This trend was to increase dramatically during the next few years. In 1939, 412 963 tons of china-clay was exported out of a total of 707 967 tons produced. [21] At that time there were 41 clay companies, but when they failed to reach agreement on a wartime concentration scheme the Board of Trade stepped in and reduced the number of pits by half. By 1941 only 23 pits remained in operation and 60 per cent of the workforce had left the industry. Production of china clay fell to a third of its pre-war output. [22] Exports in that year dwindled to 116 622 tons through the loss of European markets, and export to America was difficult because of a shortage of shipping. Soon exports to the USA went via Avonmouth or Bristol to avoid the hazardous English Channel. These shipments peaked at 67 195 tons in 1941, but subsequently declined to a paltry 213 tons by 1945. [23]

The number of ships carrying china clay leaving the port of Fowey dropped from a pre-war peak of 893 vessels in 1936 to just 45 in 1941. It was a similar story at Par from where a total of 593 clay ships had sailed in 1937, dropping to 66 in 1945. At the clay port of Charlestown a very limited trade continued, with two berths reserved for incoming and outgoing vessels, but only 17 ships left with clay between 1942 and 1945. The total for 1937 had been 307 vessels. [24]

While many of the workforce went off to war or found employment in related industries, the clay companies were forced to diversify. In July 1940 ECLP were advertising concrete block air-raid shelters, which were designed for six persons and could be erected quickly, at a cost of £20 upwards. Also available was the 'Duchy Concrete Silo', being marketed in support of the campaign of the Minister of Agriculture and Fisheries. [25]

Other local companies also had to adapt to war work. When planes crashed mobile repair units were soon on the scene. Based at St Eval and consisting of members from each trade, they travelled throughout the county visiting crash sites. Serviceable components, weapons and ammunition were too valuable to be wasted. The wreckage would be returned to St Eval's large scrapyard, leaving nothing at the scene.

HTP Motors (Hosken, Trevithick & Polkinhorn) of Truro, who before the war had dealt in cars and commercial vehicles, now became a Government-approved agent, but also gave over its workshops (now the Pannier Market on Lemon Quay) for the repair of Spitfire components. About 100 people, with a variety of skills and experience, worked on the smaller items such as tailplanes, flaps and rudders which could be removed easily from the aircraft. Men and women worked alongside each other in the crowded workshop. Under strict security, the repairs had to be done quickly but accurately to get the planes back into service as soon as possible. Over 10 000 Spitfire sub-assemblies and components were repaired in HTP's Truro workshop. [26] Other HTP workshops serviced anti-aircraft guns, army vehicles and equipment.

Meanwhile work went on around the clock at Charlestown Foundry, which took on staff from the ailing china-clay industry. They assisted in the construction of components for tanks and armoured cars, and later joined with Falmouth Docks in the construction of parts for the Mulberry Harbours, augmenting the main work undertaken in the Thames Estuary, Pegwell Bay in Kent, and Southampton (See Chapter 9). Falmouth Docks & Engineering Co. Ltd was kept busy servicing Royal Navy vessels such as minesweepers, as well as providing emergency repairs and bunkering facilities for larger craft.

Other docks and boatyards also played a vital role in the war effort. At Par Docks the hulls of minesweepers were constructed by Frank Curtis of Looe, who also ran a boatyard at Totnes in Devon. Smaller yards, such as W. Frazier & Son of Mevagissey, closed at the outbreak of war, the workforce transferring to Par. Here the larger minesweepers were built outside, five at a time. These were 140 feet in length and of timber construction so that they could avoid detection by magnetic mines. Smaller Fairmile motor launches were con-

The big raids on Germany continue. British war plants share with the R.A.F. credit for these giant operations.

THE ATTACK BEGINS IN THE FACTORY

WOMEN OF BRITAIN
COME INTO THE FACTORIES
ASK AT ANY EMPLOYMENT EXCHANGE FOR ADVICE AND FULL DETAILS

The attack begins in the factory (above). *Urging women to do their bit, not just at home, but in the factories as well* (above right).

PUBLIC RECORD OFFICE

structed under cover. At 115 feet in length, they were double-skinned with a layer of canvas in between. The frames and keels for each hull were supplied as prefabricated components by the Fairmile Marine Company near London. The kit for each vessel was delivered in six boxes, each designed to fit in the back of a 15-ton lorry. A local fisherman was awarded the contract to tow the completed hulls to Charlestown, where they were fitted out and typically 500 bhp diesel engines installed. In 1943 the Admiralty called for W. Frazier & Son to re-open. They then constructed 65-foot Motor Fishing Vessels (MFVs) and naval pinnaces. [27] P. Mitchell & Sons of Portmellon near Mevagissey also built this type of craft, usually 45 feet in length.

The local fishing industry was greatly curtailed as a result of the war. Young men and members of the Royal Naval Reserve (RNR) were called up, leaving the older men to carry on the work. Despite the demand for their freshly landed catches they mainly pursued coastal fishing, being anxious about straying too far from their home ports. Their fears may have been justified; after the fishing boat *Pride of the West* from Mevagissey was machine-gunned by an enemy plane, the elderly crew were too shaken to put to sea for several days. [28]

CHAPTER 4 – REFERENCES

(PC = Personal Communication)

[1] Winston Churchill, speech to the House of Commons, 20 August 1940.

[2] *Royal Cornwall Gazette*, 17 July 1940, p. 3.

[3] *Daily Sketch*, 29 August 1940, p. 3.

[4] *The Wartime Kitchen and Garden* (1993), Jennifer Davies, p. 17.

[5] *Royal Cornwall Gazette*, 13 March 1940, p. 4.

[6] Ibid.

[7] *Royal Cornwall Gazette*, 3 April 1940, p. 3.

[8] *The Wartime Kitchen and Garden* (1993), Jennifer Davies, p. 6.

[9] *Royal Cornwall Gazette*, 5 June 1940, p. 1.

[10] *Royal Cornwall Gazette*, 18 December 1940, p. 3.

[11] *Royal Cornwall Gazette*, 21 February 1940, p. 3.

[12] *The Wartime Kitchen and Garden* (1993), Jennifer Davies, p. 81.

[13] PC: Mr Peirone Ferruccio of Turin.

[14] *The Cornish Mineral Industry* (1989), Jack Trounson, p. 33.

[15] *The Cornish Mineral Industry* (1989), Jack Trounson, p. 18.

[16] Ibid.

[17] *The Cornish Mineral Industry* (1989), Jack Trounson, p. 20.

[18] *Castle-an-Dinas 1916–1957* (2001), Tony Brooks, p. 46 and 137.

[19] *A Miner's Tale – The Story of Howard Mankee* (1988), J.A. Buckley, p. 62.

[20] *A History of the Cornish China-Clay Industry* (1966), R.M. Barton, p. 194.

[21] *Board of Trade Working Party Reports – China-Clay* (1948), Appendix I, p. 58.

[22] Ibid.

[23] *Board of Trade Working Party Reports – China-Clay* (1948), Appendix V, p. 62.

[24] *Board of Trade Working Party Reports – China Clay* (1948), Appendix IX, p. 61.

[25] *Royal Cornwall Gazette*, 17 July 1940, p. 1.

[26] *Aviation in Cornwall* (1997), Peter London, p. 55.

[27] PC: Mr W.A. Frazier.

[28] Ibid.

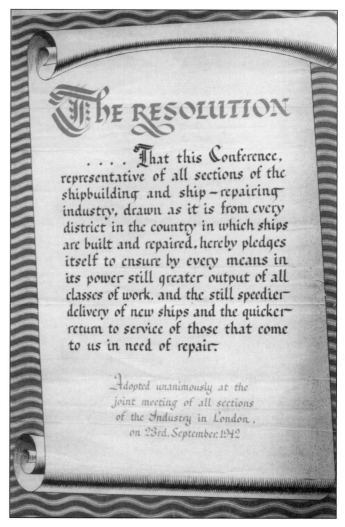

Two posters that once adorned the walls of W. Frazier and Son's boatyard at Mevagissey, urging greater production. They were rescued when the yard closed in 1977 (above).

Time spent in the docks was wasted time (above right).

THE BATTLE OF BRITAIN
AND BEYOND

What General Weygand called the 'Battle of France' is over. I expect that the Battle of Britain is about to begin. Upon this battle depends the survival of Christian civilization. Upon it depends our own British life and the long continuity of our institutions and our Empire... Let us therefore brace ourselves to our duty, and so bear ourselves that, if the British Commonwealth and its Empire lasts for a thousand years, men will still say, 'This was their finest hour'.

CHURCHILL [1]

Hitler did not court confrontation with Britain and with the fall of France he hoped to turn his attention eastwards. However, when overtures for peace came to nought, on 16 July 1940 the Fuehrer issued Directive No.16 and launched plans for *Operation Seelöwe* (Sea Lion), the invasion of Britain. His generals had differing ideas about the focus of the invasion, the army favouring a broad front between Ramsgate and Lyme Regis, whilst the naval chiefs favoured a narrow assault between Folkstone and Eastbourne. Cornwall might not have been considered because it was too far from the capital and an invading force could find itself vulnerable to a counter-attack.

From the defenders' point of view, however, there was a fear that an invasion could be mounted from the French-held channel ports. It was felt that the Germans could take advantage of Cornwall's physical geography, being a long narrow peninsula bisected by river estuaries. The enemy would only need to gain a bridgehead and capture some fifteen or twenty miles of land to cut off part of the county. The threat was considered serious enough so that in August and September 1940 dawn and dusk patrols were flown each day along the south coast using Lysanders from 225 Squadron and 16 Squadron operating from Roborough, Plymouth.

One thing the Germans were agreed upon was the need to eliminate the RAF's ability to attack an invasion force. Hitler's Directive No.15 issued on 13 July stated that the RAF would have to be eliminated prior to an invasion. This task fell on Herman Goering's Luftwaffe, and reinforced by Directive No.17 of 1 August which ordered them 'to crush the British Air Force by every means possible.' Goering responded, declaring 2 August 'Eagle Day'.

Although the Battle of Britain is supposed to have officially begun on 10 August and concluded on 31 October, as so often happens in wartime, engagements took place, and men and aircraft were lost, before and after these dates. Indeed, on 1 July Convoy Jumbo was attacked off Plymouth by Ju87s, and for St Eval the battle started early, when on 8 July Spitfires of 234 Squadron were scrambled to repel Ju88s which were attacking another convoy in the Western Approaches. On the same day the naval barracks at Devonport were the target of a bombing raid by 70 enemy planes.

Construction of the airfield at St Eval had begun in 1938 for Coastal Command to operate anti-submarine patrols, the base officially opening on 2 October 1939. Initially, outdated Ansons of 217 Squadron were used, followed by Hornet Moth biplanes, Whitleys and Beaufort torpedo bombers. 234 Squadron's Spitfires were later augmented by Hurricanes of 238 Squadron, which were better suited to night flying.

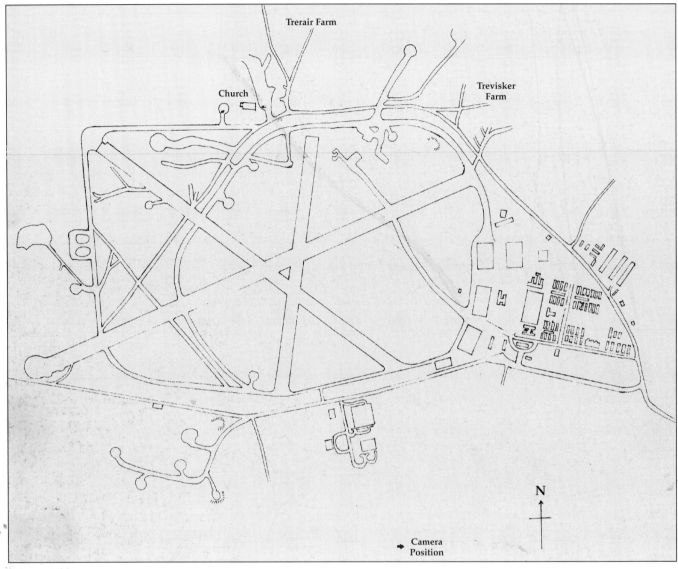

RAF St Eval

St Eval was also the base for a small but elite group of pilots who were responsible for aerial photography. Previously known as the Photographic Development Unit, on 8 June 1940 it was renamed the Photographic Reconnaissance Unit, or PRU, and brought under Coastal Command No.16. Then, following the appointment of Wing Commander Geoffrey Tuttle as Commanding Officer later that month, A Flight was formed on 1 July and sent to Wick in Scotland from where they could monitor Norwegian ports now in enemy control, while B Flight was sent to St Eval on 3 July to watch over the west coast of France. Meanwhile C and D Flights operated from Heston, their original base, along with E Flight which was responsible for training.

The pilots were chosen according to their flying and navigational abilities as well as their competence with camera equipment – not to mention their ability to withstand very cold conditions. Usually operating alone, they regu-

St Eval Church, once the centre of the hamlet of Churchtown until the cottages were demolished in 1938–39 to make way for the airfield.

St Eval Church watches over the abandoned runways of the once busy airfield. The tower was used as a lookout post as well as being a beacon for pilots.

larly flew out over the Atlantic or Bay of Biscay, gathering photographic reconnaissance of naval strength, invasion preparations, possible targets or the success of bombing campaigns. It was lonely and dangerous work; 14 pilots from St Eval's PRU were killed and two more were shot down and captured by the enemy.

To carry out these tasks they flew specially adapted 'high speed' aircraft that had been stripped of weapons and had had rivets and joints smoothed over. In this form they were able to fly at high altitudes to avoid enemy

Surviving buildings at St Eval, looking south towards RAF St Mawgan.

St Eval airfield in 1940. This example of a PRU aerial photograph is orientated towards the north with the church in the top centre, to the right of a brightly lit dispersal shown in the bottom photograph on p. 69.

WESTERN MORNING NEWS

planes. Most were Spitfires, camouflaged in a curious assortment of colour schemes including cream, duck-egg green, light blue and even pale pink. With the introduction of the Spitfire PRIV in April 1941 the planes were painted a darker cerulean blue, known as 'PR blue'. Tear-drop windows were added to the sides of the cockpit canopy to improve visibility and extra fuel tanks were fitted. The fuel capacity steadily increased, along with their operational range, as the Spitfires were developed from the PRIA through to the PRIV and PRXI.

They mainly used F24 cameras with a format of five inches by five inches, but in January 1942 the F52 was introduced for higher altitude photography, with an increased format of eight and a half inches by seven inches. Various camera positions were used on the aircraft, including facing them forwards and sideways in the wings and using fuselage mountings for both vertical and oblique projections. Processing and interpretation was carried out at the Photographic Interpretation Unit at Wembley by a range of experts, as well as at Danesfield House at Medmenham in Buckinghamshire. After the Wembley unit was bombed in October 1940, Danesfield House was then called the Central Interpretation Unit.

One such plane that operated from St Eval was a Spitfire Mk.I, serial number R7116, bought by the people of St Austell in 1940. Posters had been displayed in public places, such as outside the Odeon cinema in the town, urging people to contribute towards 'their' Spitfire. Such campaigns were successfully run in several towns, including Truro, Camborne and Redruth, St Ives and the Isles of Scilly. The £5000 necessary to purchase a Spitfire was raised, and from 20 January 1942 it flew 74 operations with 140 Squadron. Then on 8 November 1942, while photographing Guernsey, it was attacked by a squadron of FW190s and was shot down. Australian Pilot Officer Norman Amos was not injured by his crash into the sea, but was captured and became a prisoner of war. [2]

The PRU flew 30 successful sorties from St Eval in September 1940. [3] At a time when an invasion seemed imminent, daily reports of the build-up of any invasion fleet were vital. Between the nights of 13/14 and 23/24 nightly raids were made on Channel ports by Bomber Command.

From 12 August Hitler and Goering changed their tactics, diverting their attention away from Channel shipping to mount attacks on airfields. These

St Austell's Spitfire, used by the Photographic Reconnaissance Unit (PRU). It is pictured taking off from St Eval in 1941. It would be shot down over the Channel Islands. Note the teardrop window on the cockpit cowl added to improve visibility.

WESTERN MORNING NEWS

On 22 March 1943 the U-boat U-665 *was spotted by the crew of a Whitley V of No. 10 Operational Training Unit (OTU) from St Eval. Using six depth charges the enemy submarine was sunk with all hands. She had been returning from her first operational voyage.*

were, after all, large and clearly defined targets which were hard to defend. Between July 1940 and November 1941 St Eval and its vicinity was attacked on 17 occasions. [4] Measures were taken to protect them. They could be 'blacked-out' if there were reports of enemy aircraft. They were also provided with Q-sites; dummy airfields laid out with lights on nearby land which could lure the enemy to the wrong location. St Eval was provided with such a Q-site at Denzell Downs, moorland a short distance to the south-east of the actual aerodrome. This proved effective on the night of 26/27 August 1940 when the dummy airfield was the subject of a concerted attack that lasted for several hours but spared the real station. Dummy windmills were even built at Predannack in an attempt to confuse the enemy! It was felt that six HeIIIs might have used an old windmill nearby to aid their navigation during a raid on the incomplete airfield in April 1941. However such measures did not prevent two further attacks later in the year on this ill-equipped and dreary base.

Predannack airfield, now a satellite of post-war Culdrose.

Blast pens were constructed near the perimeter tracks of airfields to protect the vulnerable aircraft. Originally built of sandbags, they covered rudimentary brick shelters which afforded protection for air and ground crews whilst they were in this remote and exposed area. The examples at Perranporth are the only ones known to have survived; later types had earth banks with a shelter to the rear. Defensive HQs – half-buried concrete bunkers – were also built, the example at Perranporth being further protected by three pillboxes on its seaward side. More retaliatory measures would soon be provided by estab-

Land's End (St Just) Airport control tower. After the outbreak of war mainland Britain's most westerly airfield maintained a sporadic service to the Isles of Scilly until November 1941, when it was stopped following the loss of a plane.

Blast pen R6 used to protect aircraft at Perranporth. Towards the northern end of the airfield, this is one of the earliest types with sandbag walls and a shelter at the front. It is one of few still extant.

Blast pen R3 in the south-west corner of the airfield at Perranporth was built six months later than the above and was constructed with earth walls with a shelter at the rear.

lishing anti-aircraft batteries and machine-gun posts behind rings of sandbags. Counter-attacks were also mounted by designated squadrons. Then in September, Goering once again changed tactics by launching attacks on London, giving Cornwall a temporary respite.

By 17 September, with the RAF undefeated, and with his invasion fleet being targeted nightly, Hitler postponed *Operation Sea Lion* for a month. On 12 October a further postponement was announced. Then in January 1941, with the focus of the war shifting, the Fuehrer finally abandoned the idea of an invasion altogether. Enemy tactics changed. U-boats could be used to sink vessels that were providing Britain with vital provisions, thereby starving the country into submission.

During the spring of 1941 the capital ships *Scharnhorst* and *Gneisenau* were in dry dock at Brest, and daily reconnaissance by two planes of the PRU had been monitoring the work, for once returned to operations they would continue to devastate merchant shipping. After a previous attack *Gneisenau* had been moved to the outer harbour so that an unexploded bomb could be safely defused. Here

Perranporth Airfield. A unique example of a Second World War fighter station, with the defensive structures intact (opposite).

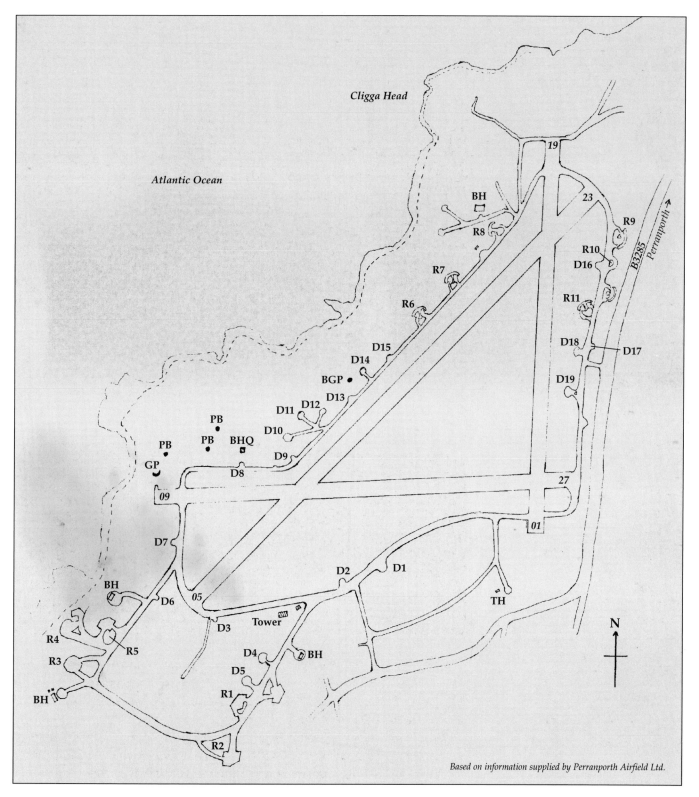

Based on information supplied by Perranporth Airfield Ltd.

RAF Perranporth (Trevellas)

DISPERSAL / DEFENSIVE STRUCTURES KEY

R = Pens and shelters.
D = Hardstanding dispersals.
BH = Blister Hangar site.
TH = Teesside Hangar site.
BGP = Bofors gun pit.
PB = Pill boxes.
GP = Gun post.
BHQ = Defensive battle headquarters.

EXPLANATIONS

Pens at the north end of the field (R6–11) are the earliest type – the only examples in existence. They have sandbag walls and shelter at the front.

Pens at south and west, built 6 months later, have earth walls and shelter at rear.

Battle HQ has defensive pill boxes to west.

Gun practice with a Lewis gun at Perranporth in 1942 (above). Swinging a Bofors anti-aircraft gun into action, again at Perranporth in 1942 (above right).

G. MITCHELL

PRU photographs revealed that the battleship was now more vulnerable. On 6 April an attack was ordered using Beauforts of 22 Squadron flying out of St Eval. For his courageous determination to press home the attack when support failed to materialise, and for which there could be only one outcome, the pilot, Flying Officer Kenneth Campbell, was awarded a posthumous VC.

To keep tabs on enemy shipping in the port of Brest, *Operation Stopper* was instigated using PRU Spitfires from 543 Squadron and Hudsons from 224 Squadron. On 11 February 1942 a PRU Spitfire glimpsed through the clouds the repaired *Gneisenau,* along with the *Scharnhorst* and the heavy cruiser *Prinz Eugen,* preparing to leave harbour. However, because of enemy action, poor weather and bad luck, the ships slipped out under cover of darkness and it took twelve hours before they could be located. So serious was this failure that a Board of Enquiry was set up, but it found that no individual was to blame.

On 19 October 1942 B Flight of the PRU changed to A Flight of 543 Squadron, one of only five PRU squadrons operating in Britain. Later, in June 1943, 543 Squadron, along with the other PRUs in Britain were brought under No.106 (PR) Wing, and 543 Squadron was disbanded in October. With rationalisation over they continued to run six Spitfires until 1944, then Mosquitoes were provided. Ansons, Blenheims and Hudsons were also used by some squadrons. By now they were providing vital reconnaissance of enemy-held territory in preparation for the Allied landings.

Regular and accurate meteorological reports were vital in war-time, especially in days before aircraft had the advantages of modern 'all weather' capability. Therefore another small group of pilots was given the task of gathering weather data. One such group was also based at St Eval.

The 1404 Meteorological Reconnaissance Flight (MRF) were initially given three Blenheim aircraft and three crews. The planes were equipped with extra fuel tanks located in the bomb bay, making them capable of flights of up to 500 miles from base. The nature of the job meant that the planes were often operating in extreme conditions. Weather-recording apparatus was unsophisticated; crews used an instrument similar to a wet and dry thermometer and a barometer, as well as making observations of cloud patterns and wind direction.

In March 1942 the Flight was equipped with four new Hudsons. These aircraft, modified from the civil Lockheed 14 Super Electra and now fitted with seven machine guns, replaced the old Avro Anson. At times, old aircraft that were not fit for active service were pressed into use. A Lancaster 'Airies' was modified so that it no longer had the protection afforded by gun turrets or camouflage and conducted experimental navigational flights over Polar regions where a traditional compass was inoperable. Halifaxes and later Flying Fortresses, with the range to reach the Azores, were also used. Besides monitoring the weather, the MFR undertook a large number of anti-submarine operations. In fact their techniques proved so successful that they were later adopted by other units. [5]

The planes were expected to fly whatever the weather conditions. It is therefore not surprising that casualty rates within the unit were relatively high; 21 men were lost whilst gathering important meteorological information for planning operations. [6] One of the planes lost with all hands was a Hudson, which became disorientated in fog as it searched for its base and crashed into cliffs at Kellan Head near Port Quin.

Actually combating this most capricious of conditions therefore became an issue. Whenever possible operations could not be curtailed by the weather, and planes, some often badly damaged, had to be able to return to base. One of the most dangerous hazards was fog.

St Eval was one of 18 airfields in Britain, and the only one in the West Country, to be equipped with FIDO (Fog Investigation and Dispersal Operation, but redefined in June 1945 as Fog, Intensive, Dispersal Of). Today the system may be considered crude, but the idea was to literally burn the fog from the airfields by consuming vast quantities of petrol. A row of pipes ran along each side of the runway, raised about a foot from the ground. The petrol, controlled by pumps and large valves, ran through three miles of pipework to regularly spaced burners. At a time when the fuel ration for members of the public was severely curtailed – the amount allowed depending upon one's needs – many would have been horrified at the 60 000 gallons of fuel which could be burnt in an hour along the runway.

To feed this voracious contraption two railway sidings were constructed at Shell Mex's Quintrell Downs depot. From here the fuel was dispatched in four petrol tankers, each transporting 4000 gallons at a time. According to one eyewitness at the initial trials, the system was ignited by a man walking from one burner to the next with a long taper! [7] It was extinguished by simply switching off the fuel supply. Initially the system produced a shroud of smoke denser than the original hazard, but as the burners warmed up the fires burnt cleanly and the roaring inferno dispersed the fog to a height of 300-400 feet. Certainly the contraption saved many war-time pilots before more sophisticated radar systems had been developed. At that time more faith was put in primitive but effective methods of landing aircraft in poor weather conditions. Yet ironically, FIDO was installed just after the Ground Control Approach radar (GCA) trials had finished at St Eval in October 1943.

Work to develop this secret American equipment had been going on during the summer of that year, and Davidstow Moor was chosen for testing it. This proved to be a poor choice; perpetually inclement weather meant that the GCA radar system could not be set up in order to be used to help pilots land in poor conditions! The system was therefore transferred briefly to St Eval in September. A month later the trials were moved to Northamptonshire.

Long before the war, many experiments had been carried out on radar (an acronym for radio detecting and ranging). The British in particular had seen its potential for providing an early warning system and, as early as 1934, a committee of scientists had been set up to investigate the best methods. Robert Watson-Watt's team from the National Physical Laboratory successfully completed experiments using a short-wave transmitter, so in 1937 they began to set up the Chain early-warning system along the Thames estuary. By early 1940 this had been extended to cover the whole coast from the Firth of Forth to the Solent. The following months saw it covering the entire south-west.

Air Ministry 'Experimental Stations' were established which consisted of Chain Home (CH) transmitters strung between 350-foot high towers, and Chain Home Low (CHL) receivers using 250-foot towers. Cornwall had three CHLs: at Drytree on the Lizard Peninsula (now Goonhilly Satellite Earth Station); Rame Head; and at Carnanton adjacent to RAF St Mawgan near the north coast.

Details of approaching enemy aircraft could be sent by telephone to the Group Centre at Stanmore, north of London. The 'plot and tell' information provided them with details of the range and bearing of the target, as well as the grid reference, which could then be re-plotted on a map at the control centre ready to coordinate a response.

Ground radar stations were also used to locate aircraft and surface vessels, which could then alert gun batteries to take appropriate action. This system was augmented by the work of the Observer Corps, who could identify individual aircraft and determine whether they were friend or foe. (See Chapter 2.)

Finding enough billets for aircrews was often a problem. This became even more acute at St Eval after the living quarters of the aircrew were destroyed in a raid. A former navigator with 1404 MRF recalls being de-briefed at an emergency operations room relocated in nearby agricultural buildings after one raid in 1941. [8] Various local hotels were pressed into service including the Trevelgue Hotel at Porth, taken over by 502 (Auxiliary) Squadron as their Officers' Mess, the Gull Rock Hotel, Porth for WAAFs and The White House, Tregurrian for WAAF officers. The Watergate Bay Hotel was an Officers' Mess and later married quarters, while the cottages across the road – now gone – were used by PRU pilots. NCOs were billeted at Bedruthan Steps Hotel and Treyarnon Bay Hotel.

Pressure to find billets did not just come from existing airmen. Many pilots and aircrew received their training in Cornwall. After passing entry examinations the new recruits, mostly in their late teens or early twenties, were sent to the Aircrew Receiving Centre at Lord's Cricket Ground in London (only a short distance away from Campbell Street School, evacuated to Cornwall in 1939 – see Chapter 7). They would have spent about six weeks there undertaking 'square-bashing'; carrying out drill to instil discipline and other basic training. From there they were sent to Initial Training Wings (ITWs) located at Newquay, Torquay, Aberystwyth, Scarborough or St Andrew's.

8 Initial Training Wing, with its headquarters at the Trebarwith Hotel in Newquay, became operational in late 1940. Mr R.C. Extence recalls that the HQ's small manual telephone switchboard was located in the bathroom next to the Commanding Officer's Office and this meant that the person on night duty slept in the bath! All telex messages came through RAF St Eval. There were about 200 permanent staff, plus civilian cleaners, storekeepers and so on. Some

of the cooks were conscripts who had been working in London West End hotels, so the ITW enjoyed excellent cuisine. Hotels in Island Crescent were mainly used to billet permanent staff, and many of the hotels at the western end of Newquay were requisitioned by the Air Ministry. Buildings like the Cosy Nook Theatre (since replaced by an aquarium) and Camelot Cinema served as assembly halls and classrooms. A similar situation arose at the eastern end of Newquay where 7 ITW was based. [9]

Each Wing had about 200 trainees a week on six-week courses, giving a total of 2400 trainees in Newquay. There were also a large number of army personnel in the town. The recruits were instructed in navigation, communication using Morse code and Aldis lamps, as well as in the use of machine guns. Apprentices wore a pale blue flash in their glengarrys and an apprentice wheel on their arm until they reached the age of eighteen or completed their training.

Usually on alternate weeks the whole course would be sent abroad for their flying training at Flying Training Schools in Canada, USA, Rhodesia or South Africa. Mr Extence, then a seventeen-year-old apprentice, was responsibe for making their travel arrangements which meant issuing rail warrants, leave passes and ration cards for their embarkation leave, as well as arranging the rail travel for the 200 involved to their embarkation point in either Liverpool or Glasgow. He recalls that the GWR usually added two coaches to the local train to Par where they would be detached and then joined to the appropriate main-line train. At times the embarkation date would be brought forward which would mean sending 200 telegrams recalling the airmen from leave!

CHAPTER 5 – REFERENCES

(PC = Personal Communication)
[1] Winston Churchill, Hansard, 18 June 1940, col. 60.
[2] PC: Mr F. Harper.
[3] The Battle of Britain (1990), Michael Bowyer, p. 183.
[4] RAF St Eval 1939–1945 (2000), Frank Harper and Ian Shepherd, p. 5.
[5] PC: Mr J.A. Stephens
[6] RAF St Eval 1939–1945 (2000), Frank Harper and Ian Shepherd, p. 20.
[7] PC: Mr M. Lyne.
[8] PC: Mr J.A. Stephens.
[9] PC Mr R.C. Extence.

Towan Beach, Newquay during the summer of 1943. Three members of the Initial Training Wing chat to two servicemen from the convalescent hospital at Hotel Victoria.

WESTERN MORNING NEWS

6

COVERT OPERATIONS

...set Europe ablaze.
CHURCHILL [1]

Heavily wooded valleys with mature trees overhanging secluded creeks, much of the land owned by wealthy estates who valued their privacy; such locations were ideal for mounting special operations. Unfamiliar people and vessels could come and go without attracting undue attention. The Helford River fulfilled these requirements.

Soon after the formation of the Special Operations Executive (SOE), the Helford River was chosen as a discreet base from which to mount covert operations to France. Unfortunately it was also to be an early source of antagonism between the new service and its parallel organisation, the Secret Intelligence Service (SIS), who were already responsible for intelligence-gathering behind enemy lines.

The SOE was born out of a desire 'to co-ordinate all actions, by way of subversion and sabotage, against the enemy overseas', [2] as laid out in its charter and formally approved by the War Cabinet on 22 July 1940. It took over the role previously occupied by Section D, SIS's sabotage branch, with the aim, as Churchill put it, to 'set Europe ablaze'. However, the two organisations remained at best suspicious of each other. This was in part political; SIS was answerable to Conservative ministers, whilst SOE was under the Socialist Minister for Economic Warfare, Dr Hugh Dalton, as a concession to Labour in the coalition Government; but also SOE might find itself working alongside left-wing partisans. Then of course there were professional jealousies and the needless duplication of operations. [3] This manifested itself during the early phase of operations when the RAF refused to supply planes. 'Bomber' Harris was a vociferous critic of SOE and considered that it would be a waste of resources. The solution appeared to be a sea-going operation.

The man in charge of this Cornish operation was Commander Frank Slocum RN, a senior SIS officer. He in turn gave the task of finding a suitable base from which to mount clandestine operations to Gerald Holdsworth of SOE Holdsworth had just had a lucky escape from a failed operation in Sweden. He had an interesting background, having been a rubber planter in Borneo, then a film producer. His work in the advertising department had caught the attention of Section D who initially asked him to go to Norway posing as a herring buyer. He had scouted for suitable amphibious landing sites around Bergen. From there he had been sent to Stockholm to assist in the sabotage of the iron-ore port of Oxelosund. Before the explosives were set, his fellow-conspirator, Alexander Rickman from Section D's Scandinavian Section, had been arrested by the Swedish police and Holdsworth had been forced to seek sanctuary at the British Legation, before finding safe passage to England via Finland.

Holdsworth chose the Helford River and took up residence at 'Ridifarne' near Port Navas, overlooking the river. This was the summer retreat of the Bickford-Smith family. William Bickford-Smith had developed the miners' safety fuse, now ironically to be used for triggering explosive devices by SOE. Here he was able to accommodate boat crews and agents. As the operation expanded he acquired another house nearby, Pedn-Billy, which benefited from a thatched boathouse.

Port Navas Creek and Budock Vean. Pedn-Billy can be seen on the right, with the thatched boathouse in the foreground partly obscured by a tree.

Among his subordinates was Lieutenant Francis Brooks Richards, Holdsworth's deputy. As a young naval officer he had been badly injured in an explosion on a minesweeper and had subsequently transferred to SOE. They were joined by Nigel Warington-Smyth, a boat designer and yachtsman. His skills would be employed to develop surf boats for landing agents, testing them at Praa Sands. Boat crews included Bunny Newton, a Guernsey fisherman who had been recommended by Ian Fleming; a Breton fisherman called Pierre Guillet; as well as a few locals and adventurers. For all of them secrecy was paramount, even when talking with family and friends.

A fleet of boats was soon assembled. The principal operational vessel was a 65-foot Breton tunnyman named the *Mutin* (the *Rebel*). If the genuine articles were unavailable, craft were built or adapted to resemble French fishing boats, but fitted with two 650bhp. Hall-Scott petrol engines, providing them with an uncharacteristic speed of over 25 knots. There was also a 41-foot seaplane tender borrowed from the R.A.F., designated *RAF360*, capable of

maintaining a speed of 22 knots, and a 50-foot trawler, the *N51* which operated out of the advanced base on the Isles of Scilly. The *Sunbeam 2*, a 3-masted schooner which had formerly been the private yacht of Lord Runciman, was painted grey and became the nautical HQ of Nigel Warington-Smyth after he took over command in the summer of 1943. Together this motley fleet was known as the Helford Flotilla.

However, once assembled, it can be argued that full use was never made of the Helford Flotilla. Operations were soon restricted as Slocum and SIS were concerned about the infiltration of their own agents, and there were fears of increasing German E-boat patrols in the Channel.[4] Despite this, during the winter of 1940–41, a number of night-time landings were made on the Brittany coast in order to drop or pick up agents, supplies or weapons. Sabotage equipment was also employed, including plastic explosives in lumps of coal or incendiary devices disguised as rats. They were used in operations to disable railway tracks, marshalling yards or power stations.

The boat crews would work in darkness. Once near the French coast agents would transfer to camouflaged kayaks to paddle ashore. They had to face the risk of mines on the beach, or a concealed reception party waiting somewhere in the dark. Ashore, they would gather information or deliver the so-called Helford containers. Constructed of aluminium, these canisters had hinged lids and shoulder straps like a rucksack so they could be carried on the back, thus leaving the agent's hands free. Later, flat-bottomed plywood tenders were developed by Lieutenant Richards at Portmellon to replace the canoes, after the Germans discovered some hidden near the shore.

The return journey was also fraught with danger. Locating the mother ship was often difficult, so luminous balls were developed so they could see the returning canoeists. There was still the risk of being intercepted by E-boats or patrolling aircraft. Indeed, on one occasion the *Mutin* was machine-gunned by a German plane and her engineer was killed – despite the use of RAF wireless sets to trick the enemy into looking for a plane rather than a boat.

Some of the operations were successful, others less so. In February 1942 a Soviet agent, Anna Uspenskaya, was landed in France but, tragically, she was captured by the Germans and shot. More successful was the mission to bring the French Intelligence Officer, Colonel Gilbert Renault-Routre, known as 'Remy', and his family back from France. He brought with him a map of German coastal defences in France, acquired by a painter and decorator who had audaciously smuggled it out of the German headquarters in a roll of wall-paper. The brothers, Joel and Yves Letac, were taken to Brittany on board the seaplane tender *RAF360* and got ashore by kayak. Joel helped organise the sabotage of the Pessac electric power station at Merignac near Bordeaux in an operation code-named *Josephine B*.

The last operation undertaken by the Helford Flotilla was the retreaval of 32 people, including many airmen, from Brittany on Christmas Day 1943. To facilitate this a specially constructed 26-foot surf boat, SN6, was towed across the Channel by *MGB318* stationed in Falmouth. The smaller vessel was then used to transfer the men to the waiting MGB (Motor Gun Boat).

Other vessels operated out of Cornish ports besides the Helford Flotilla. French fishing boats found refuge here following the fall of France. Several were used by the Free French Navy as well as the British intelligence services for clandestine operations. They had the advantage of being able to rendezvous with the genuine French tunny fleet, which continued to operate from occupied ports, and could therefore exchange information, or relay agents or equipment whilst in the fishing grounds. They were designated the Inshore Patrol Flotilla, but their role was kept secret and when in port they were moored away from other vessels and no-one without authority was allowed aboard, even if it meant resorting to force.

There were almost 40 French fishing vessels moored in Fowey at any given time. Three of these were used for clandestine operations and were moored on the far side of the river at Pont Pill, a little downstream from Polruan. The *Roger Juliette* of 169 gross tons had been seized by the Royal Navy in Belfast in July 1940, the *St Denise Louise* of 42 gross tons had taken part in the evacuation from Dunkirk and the *Trebouliste* of 119 tons, which had escaped from France. Arriving in Fowey in January 1941, the *Trebouliste* was renamed *MFV2032* (Motor Fishing Vessel). The *Roger Juliette* was used as an auxiliary patrol vessel at Falmouth until January 1941, before going to Fowey in June 1942. That November she was joined by *St Denise Louise*, now re-named *MFV2014*. [5]

The Free French also used a small dockyard at Mylor, owned by the Admiralty. It was used as a secret base for shipping agents to France, again using French fishing boats. Locals recall French sailors coming ashore. [6] A small shed at the end of the jetty which had served as a sail store was even occasionally used as a mortuary when things went wrong. This building is now the site of the new Mylor Yacht Club. Initially such operations would have been undertaken independently of SOE's F Section, because, after all, the British organisation didn't exist!

The role of seaborne operations had declined by 1942, to be replaced by airborne operations. A Wing Commander at that time recalls, 'several special flights were constantly being flown on hush-hush missions', [7] from St Eval. May 1941 marked SOE's first successful parachute mission into France, and four months later the first Lysander pick-up took place, code-named *Operation Levée*. Although successful, this had its limitations; the Lysander was a small, 870hp single-engined aircraft which was easy to handle but had the disadvantage of only having a small payload. Also, it was realised that larger gunboats based in Dartmouth were more suitable and these undertook some 40 operations. HMS *Fidelity* was being operated out of Gibraltar and was used to carry both SIS and SOE agents to the less secure Vichy-controlled Mediterranean coast.

With the Germans on the defensive rather than the offensive, and as new theatres of war opened up, the Helford Flotilla was of less importance and in the autumn of 1942 Gerald Holdsworth and many of his men transferred their operation to Algeria. Then in the summer of 1943, SIS and SOE operations were combined on the Helford, under the command of Nigel Warington-Smyth.

A covert operation to Algeria, the full truth of which will probably never come to light, ended tragically. Early on the morning of 17 April 1944 a twin-engined Warwick Mk.1, *BV247*, of 525 Squadron based at Lyneham in Wiltshire, was preparing to take off from St Mawgan. Shortly before it did so it is believed that a package was taken on board and placed in the cockpit. It was one of a batch of 12 Warwicks which had been specially furnished as civilian aircraft, for besides this mysterious package and the aircrew, the transport plane carried a group of high-ranking military advisers and linguists. They included two French officers on the way to join General de Gaulle, four SOE officers and a Russian-speaking MI6 officer en route to Yugoslavia to meet up with General Tito. The plane's destination was Maison Blanche, Algeria, via Gibraltar [8]. The Allies had re-taken Algeria in November 1942 during *Operation Torch*, and Algiers was now the seat of the French Committee of National Liberation. The Americans had also set up small deception units at their bases in Algiers and Tunis. The secret agents were prepared for covert insertion into Southern Europe where they could pave the way for the forthcoming invasion.

The passengers carried gold coins, secret documents and supposedly had with them crates of gold to pay partisans fighting in the Balkans. It was certainly common practice for airmen in Algeria to carry an escape kit containing silk maps, a compass, matches in a waterproof pouch, survival rations and a sum of money including gold coins, also in a sealed packet. On missions to countries where they might be regarded as infidels they also carried what was referred to as a 'gooley chit', a request for fair treatment and assistance in being returned to an Allied unit, written in both Arabic and English. [9] Agents were also provided with a tiny cyanide tablet. On a similar operation in June 1942 an SOE agent had been given a silk belt containing 500 000 francs for the French Resistance. He was arrested before the donation could be delivered. [10]

The take-off was observed by a member of the Home Guard. Some distance off Watergate Bay the plane crashed. The eye-witness later reported seeing an

A silk escape map. A map of Greece is on the reverse.

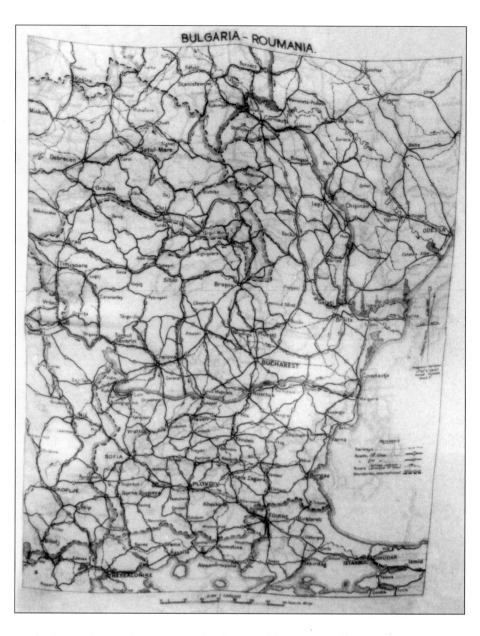

explosion and was able to give the time and location. All 18 people on board were killed.

Meanwhile SOE members working on a motor gun boat in the Adriatic with Tito received orders to go to Trieste to meet the Warwick and collect the gold bullion. They were to be disappointed. [11]

Air Sea Rescue Launch 2641 arrived at the crash scene from Padstow, but found nothing; nor did a US survey vessel that later arrived from Ilfracombe. Some years ago a team of Norwegian divers found parts of the Warwick, as well as the remains of an unknown B-17 only 60 metres away! To date the gold – as far as anyone is aware – has never been recovered.

Yet the mystery surrounding the crash was only just beginning. Some of the men were buried in a Newquay cemetery, but as they were travelling under assumed identities there is even doubt about whether the correct names appear on one or more of their headstones. In fact, the pilot was originally buried in Fairpark Cemetery, St Columb Minor, in a grave marked 'unknown merchant seaman'. Only after diligent detective work by some interested parties and an exhumation in 1984 was it established that the grave was that of the twenty-three-year-old Canadian Warwick pilot, Arthur Gavel.

Theories surrounding the crash include suggestions that the flight was sabotaged. There has been speculation that an atmospheric bomb had been planted on board that would explode when it reached a certain altitude. [12] Two Frenchmen on the aircraft might have held information that could have been considered a threat to the secret D-Day preparations. [13] It transpired that they had worked at Bletchley Park where they had been involved in the decoding of Enigma intercepts, and might have been considered a security risk by MI6. There were pro and anti-de Gaulle factions in the French secret service. Also, it is likely that resistance groups across occupied Europe had plans to blow up railway lines, roads and bridges to prevent the German armoured units reinforcing the invasion areas ahead of the Normandy landings and these could not be compromised.

On the other hand, and less sinister, the airworthiness of the Warwick aircraft has been called into question. The Warwick, basically an enlarged Wellington, appeared to have a poor record. Problems had been reported with the Pratt & Whitney Double Wasp engines, including some engine fires and difficulties with feathering propellers. Early Warwicks also experienced control difficulties, especially rudder balance, and this made them unpopular with their crews. [14] So the tragedy could have been the result of a simple accident with a fully-laden aircraft, full of fuel and flying in poor light. Certainly this was the line taken by the Court of Inquiry which said that the crash was due to, 'fog, engine failure or avoiding action of another aircraft causing loss of control.' Clearly these are three unrelated reasons, none of which tie up with the eye-witness report. So there does seem to have been a cover-up, for the Home Guard sergeant was not called to give evidence, little effort was made to correctly identify the body of the pilot when it was recovered, and the lifeboat crew had been sworn to keep secret their discovery of a money belt. 'For whatever reason there can be no doubt that the authorities made a deliberate attempt to mislead and ignore evidence about the Warwick's fateful last mission'. [15] The truth about why the crash happened will probably never be known.

Earlier in the war preparations had also been made in case the unthinkable happened and the Germans managed to carry out a successful invasion. A secret army was in readiness, prepared to carry out guerilla warfare against the enemy. Known as Auxiliary Units, a deliberately ambiguous title, they were made up of hand-picked volunteers. They wore Home Guard uniforms and were therefore taken as such. So successful were they at keeping their existence a secret that it was not until the 1960s that this came to light, and was even a revelation to many former Home Guard members.

The man behind this last-ditch idea was Major Colin Gubbins, an expert in guerilla warfare. In late 1941 there were 28 patrols operating in Cornwall, made up of 195 men. [16] Members of the Auxiliary Units were given special training in demolition, unarmed combat and stealth. This was undertaken at Coleshill Estate in Wiltshire, as well as Porthpean near St Austell under Captain Robin Williams. Training exercises also involved mock-attacks on various local 'targets'. Soldiers were issued with a booklet entitled *Highworth's Fertilisers* which, to the casual observer, resembled an agricultural catalogue but was in fact a handbook on explosives, timing devices and other useful information.

Captain Dingley, based in Stoke Climsland, was the senior officer, superceded by Captain Abbiss of Truro shortly before the units were stood down in November 1944, once the threat of invasion had passed.

A watchtower at Porthpean overlooking St Austell Bay. Such observation posts would have given the first visual warning of a forthcoming invasion. But was it manned by the Home Guard or Auxiliary Units?

Each unit had a hideout, usually buried beneath the ground in dense woodland, where arms and equipment were stashed, including mines, explosives and emergency supplies. They were provided with enough operational stores and rations to last for a short period only. After that time their cause would be lost. One member recalls, 'We were issued with a Sten gun, a commando knife, a .38 Smith and Wesson revolver, water purifying tablets, rum ration and three weeks supply of food.' [17]

Had a call to mobilise been made, the Auxiliary Units would have been left behind with the task of demolishing Brunel's Royal Albert Bridge over the Tamar, whilst the regular army retreated into Devon, abandoning the Duchy to the Germans and retreating to the 'General Headquarters Line' further up the country, from behind which a counter-attack could be mounted. How effective these units would have been was fortunately never put to the test.

In the event of the peninsula being cut off by an enemy invasion, contingency plans were also in place to maintain communications – using pigeons. This was a tried and tested method that had proved successful during the First World War. By now pigeons were being used by the RAF as standard equipment on all bombers and reconnaissance aircraft, as well as by the army and the intelligence services. Organised by the National Pigeon Service, the breeding and handling of the birds was undertaken by civilian pigeon fanciers who supplied some 200 000 birds nationally. Messages were written on rice paper to keep the size and weight to a minimum. Special containers designed to hold the messages were attached to the birds' legs. In three and a half years 16 554 pigeons were parachuted into enemy territory by the Army Pigeon Service. Of these 1842 are thought to have returned, often with secret messages. [18]

There was clearly an element of risk in this system. The birds had to be taken to the source of information, and this could entail being transported on bomber or reconnaissance planes, or being dropped by parachute while being incarcerated in a variety of special canisters. Some were of metal construction while one type used by the National Pigeon Service was made of cardboard; collapsable, it could carry two birds. Others were fitted with a waterproof lid which sealed on contact with the sea leaving the pigeon with half an hour's survival time. Alternatively, the birds could be released by hand from a plane, but it was found that they had to be released downwards and with their heads into the slipstream to avoid injury – and the aircraft should not be doing more than 200 knots. Many birds failed to reach their destinations; some birds were shot or injured, others were attacked by peregrine falcons. However, there were success stories.

A landing party arrived on the west coast of France in 1941 and sent back a message by pigeon. The bird, by the name of Navy Blue, reached Plymouth despite being injured. In October 1943 Royal Blue – NURP.40.GVIS.453 – was the first pigeon in the war to deliver a message from a force-landed aircraft on the continent. Both birds were awarded the Dickin Medal, two of 32 birds to receive this avian Victoria Cross.

The military, Home Guard and police all used pigeons as flying telegraphs. Two pigeons at a time were relayed every other day from Taunton, Exeter and Plymouth by dispatch riders to St Nicholas Gate Lofts in Bodmin. From there they were transferred to holding stations at Truro, Falmouth and Penzance. The system called for twenty-four-hour surveillance, so that when a message arrived, the Army Signals at Bodmin Barracks could be contacted, so that a dispatch rider could be sent to collect the message. [19]

Bodmin Barracks would go on to help the US forces create their own lofts, which the Yanks referred to as 'peanut-stands'. The Americans also undertook experiments to try to determine what made the homing pigeons return. They found that the birds were confused if released near a radio transmitting station, but concluded that, 'Signal Corps engineers offer no explanation of how this happened.' [20]

CHAPTER 6 – REFERENCES

(PC = Personal Communication)

[1] Winston Churchill's brief to SOE, 1940.

[2] *Secret War* (1992), Nigel West, p. 20.

[3] See West's *Secret War* for an in-depth look at the birth of SOE and its quarrels with SIS.

[4] *Secret War* (1992), Nigel West, p. 29.

[5] *Fowey at War* (19–), Paul Richards and Derek Reynolds, p. 33 & 37.

[6] *Falmouth's Wartime Memories* (1994), Trelawny, p. 30.

[7] Group Captain (then Wing Commander) F.C. Richardson C.B.E. quoted in *The Memories Linger On – A Collection of Reminiscences of Wartime RAF St Eval* (1989), compiled by Jean Shapland, p. 25.

[8] PC: Mr R. West (Ex A.S.R./M.C.S. Member).

[9] *Five Crashes Later* (1988), D.L. Stevenson, p. 84.

[10] *Trojan Horses – Deception Operations in the Second World War* (1991), Martin Young and Robbie Stamp, p. 76.

[11] PC: Mr R. West.

[12] Ibid.

[13] *Western Morning News,* 15 September 1993, p. 4.

[14] PC: Mr F.R. Andrew.

[15] F.R. Andrew in the Cornish Aviation Society's newsletter, December 1990.

[16] *Operation Cornwall* (1994), Viv Acton and Derek Carter, p. 50.

[17] Trevor Miners in *Perran at War* (1995), M. Edwards, p. 37.

[18] The Flying Telegraph Exhibition of Flt Lt Dan Humphries.

[19] Ibid.

[20] *The American Weekly,* 3 June 1945, p. 14.

7

THE BLITZ

In all my life I have never been treated with so much kindness as by the people who have suffered most. One would think one had brought some great benefit to them, instead of the blood and tears, the toil and sweat, which is all I ever promised. On every side, there is the cry, 'We can take it', but with it, there is also the cry, 'Give it 'em back'.

CHURCHILL [1]

The Luftwaffe's attempts to destroy the RAF were not as straightforward as German leaders had supposed; in fact, the enemy pilots often found themselves at a disadvantage, with no radar or VHF communications with command centres. Enemy bombers were having more success against airfields and military installations. The turning point came on 27 August 1940 when the RAF bombed Berlin, something that Goering had promised the Fuehrer could never happen. Enraged at the audacity, Hitler called for retaliation on London. Far more fighter planes were now deployed to protect the bombers, taking the pressure off Fighter Command at a crucial time.

Soon other cities became targets. For the moment Cornwall escaped concerted raids by large numbers of bombers, but suffered from 'tip and run' attacks, often by returning planes dropping surplus bombs or, according to one account, from nightly raids carried out from a training airfield in Brittany where German bomber pilots were instructed to bomb whenever they saw lights. [2]

On Thursday, 25 January 1941, seven Heinkel 111 bombers of Kampfgruppe 126 flew from their base in Brittany with orders to attack St Eval, St Merryn and a nearby radar station. It was almost 20:00 hours when, taking St Eval by surprise, they dropped their 250kg high explosive and incendiary bombs, as well as silent parachute mines. A number of them missed their targets, falling harmlessly onto nearby farmland. Several Hurricanes were damaged as well as buildings, including the unoccupied married quarters.

Tragically one bomb – some eye-witnesses say a 250kg bomb, others claim a parachute mine – exploded at the entrance of an air-raid shelter near the hangars, where all but those on essential duty were waiting for the all-clear. Twenty-two people were killed. After the sirens went white awnings were placed round the area, and the bodies were stretchered to a barn at neighbouring Trevisker Farm. Twelve people were later interred at St Eval churchyard, while others were buried at St Columb or taken home.

It could have been worse; not far away was the base's own bomb dump, and if that had been struck a large area could have been devastated. One unexploded bomb (UXB) was also found on the perimeter track at the end of Runway 26.

A poignant reminder of a wartime tragedy. The graves at St Eval churchyard include some of those who died on 25 January 1941.

The Devonport-based frigate HMS Veryan Bay. The 'Bay Class' also included HMS St Austell Bay.

The coat-of-arms from Bodmin's wartime Leyland fire appliance, registration number DCV 780.

MR M. LYNE

From December 1940 Plymouth became one of the targets for the so-called 'Baedeker' raids, cathedral cities listed in the German's pre-war Baedeker Tourist Guide. These reached their most devastating in March and April 1941. In towns as far away as St Austell and Newquay people looked east to the glow of the blazing city lighting up the night sky.

To help deal with the infernos, fire crews were dispatched to Plymouth from stations throughout Cornwall, as well as from the south of England. After a cold journey riding on the side of the fire tenders, exposed to the elements, the men stayed as long as a week before they were stood down. The crews ate and slept when they could. They were assisted by the Auxiliary Fire Service (AFS), though they might not have been considered equals. These volunteers, men and women, worked either full-time or part-time. In mid 1941 the AFS was combined with the regular fire service to form the National Fire Service under

Bodmin's Leyland fire appliance, supplied new in 1937, was in attendance at all the raids on Plymouth in 1940–41. In the foreground are Les Vincent (Driver), Chief Officer Lyne and Les Burton (2nd Officer).

MR M. LYNE

the Fire Services (Emergency Provision) Bill. The problem of incompatible hoses and standpipes was also addressed, as Cornish brigades had found themselves impotent when their hoses would not connect to some Plymouth water mains.

Tragically, on 21 April 1941 five volunteer firemen from Newquay were killed, whilst two others lost limbs. One of the survivors is recorded as saying, 'It was strange, because nine of us were there and the explosion killed every other one in the line. Each alternate person was all right.' [3]

On the same night, an underground shelter in Portland Square, Plymouth, received a direct hit from a high explosive bomb. Seventy-two people were killed, with only two survivors. Six Saltash AFS men were also killed whilst fighting a fire in King Street, Devonport. Such incidents reflect the horror and indiscriminate nature of aerial bombing. Between 21–25 April, during what became known as the 'Five-Night Blitz' on Plymouth, 590 people including 17 firemen were killed. [4]

With much of the city flattened and the threat of further attacks, many people fled to Saltash, Torpoint or further afield. This fresh influx of evacuees, on top of those already there, created its own problems:

The arrival in Truro on Saturday of 250 evacuees from Plymouth brought the billeting problem to a climax. [5]

Truro had already taken evacuees from London and Bristol, but they were not alone. By 22 May over 100 evacuees from Plymouth had arrived in Fowey, bringing the total number to 550, including 225 children. [6] This figure had dropped to 162 people by December, 108 of whom were from Plymouth. [7] Some 34 000 evacuees were billeted in Cornwall in 1941, [8] but clearly this figure fluctuated, depending on the perceived danger, the total number having fallen to 8620 by 1943 as many returned home. [9]

The Blitz on Plymouth had other repercussions, particularly for south-east Cornwall. If the bombers failed to find their targets the surrounding area suffered. This was graphically conveyed in the County ARP Records, which stated:

During the night of the 21st April [1941] the enemy dropped no less than 2 paramines, over 30 HEs and 4000 odd IBs [incendiary bombs] in the Saltash

Clockwise, starting from top left:
Bodmin Fire Brigade's mobile canteen, donated by the people of Ottawa, Canada, was taken to the scene of large fires for several days at a time. From left to right: Mrs Smith, Les Batten and Mrs Evelyn Lyne serve the firemen.

Note the NFS (National Fire Service) emblems on the uniforms.

Bodmin Fire Brigade being instructed in dealing with plane crashes by 'Snowy' White, Company Officer, at St Germans. Note the Morris 25 in the foreground, used for towing the mobile canteen.

Bodmin Fire Brigade parade outside St Germans House. Left to right: CO Lyne, Lord Eliot of St Germans, CO 'Snowy' White and Section Leader Champion.

Car Green and Torpoint – Mount-Edgecumbe (sic) areas. Fires were caused and upwards of 14 houses and 6 shops were damaged. 2000 IBs fell at Torpoint and a similar number at Saltash; over 400 fell between Millbrook and Mount Edgecumbe. [10]

On 23 April 1941 Mount Edgcumbe House was gutted when it was struck by incendiary bombs. The fire brigades were hampered through a lack of water, as well as by a UXB that was reported at the Torpoint Ferry entrance, causing all traffic to be stopped, proving to be 'a serious handicap for Fire Brigades from Cornwall many of whom were stopped at Liskeard and diverted to Saltash.' [11] On 23/24 April the Naval storage tanks at Thanckes, Torpoint were hit, and 'serious fires occurred for some days'. [12] Even the Royal Albert Railway Bridge was the focus of attention for the Luftwaffe. When raids did take place fire appliances were often being used in Plymouth, and the majority of people harboured in shelters were Plymothians and service personnel had been ordered out of barracks.

By 1941 Cornwall was suffering from a greater number of raids, particularly on strategic targets like ports and airfields. That year Falmouth had at least ten air raids. Fortunately several did little damage other than instil terror in many residents. A number of bombs missed the docks and fell into the sea.

When, in February 1941, an enemy plane attempted to bomb Falmouth, a parachute mine was damaged by anti-aircraft fire, causing it to miss its target and fall into the inner harbour. It failed to explode. A three-man team from the mine warfare establishment at HMS *Vernon*, Portsmouth, soon arrived on the scene. They used a special launch called *The Mouse*, which was fitted with an unusual silent propulsion system and underwater detection equipment, as well as a local diving barge to try to defuse the bomb. Finding the mine lying on the clock and detonator they attempted to move it by towing it with *The Mouse* and a motor launch. This proved unsuccessful so another dive was made. At this time the bomb exploded. The diving barge was blown to pieces and *The Mouse* sank as a huge plume of water shot into the air. Tragically, six men were killed, while another died later from his injuries. The bomb exploded on 6 March, exactly twelve days and one hour after it fell, suggesting it may have been fitted with a 'rendering active mechanism'. [13]

Cornwall suffered its share of UXBs. The Germans knew that a bomb did not have to explode to be effective. They had realised during their participation in the Spanish Civil War that if bombs failed to go off they often proved more useful, for they disrupted war work, communications and forced the civilian population to evacuate. To this end they developed bombs with time-delay fuses that could remain dormant for up to seventy-two hours. This created an even greater incidence of the UXB.

On 14 November 1941 a bomb at Bolenowe failed to explode following a raid on Redruth. The risk of the bomb being equipped with a time-delay fuse meant that a four-day movement restriction was put on the area until the Bomb Disposal Squad could make it safe. [14] Similarly, the occupants of 60 houses in Newlyn West were forced to evacuate for four days from 31 January 1941 because of four UXBs. [15] There were other problems too; on 20 March 1941 a UXB was found in a cemetery in Falmouth which had created a crater four feet in diameter and about 16 feet deep. The Home Secretary had to issue an exhumation order before it could be removed! [16]

The problem of UXBs became so acute that a U.X.B. Committee was formed. To counter the disruption they caused, bombs were placed into categories; an A1 found in a factory or work place had to be defused at any cost. Of course, there was a price to pay; on 2 October 1940 a Royal Engineers Sergeant was killed in Penzance after defusing a UXB, an oil bomb Flam 250 which had contained 16 gallons of oil until its casing had split open on impact. He had taken the central tubes, to which was attached the fuse and T.N.T. charge, in a lorry to his billet. However, whilst putting the pieces in a sack the fuse struck the ground and detonated the charge, causing him fatal injuries. [17]

A deadly game was played out between the German engineers and scientists, who were developing increasingly sophisticated and fiendish fuses, and the Bomb Disposal Squad's tactics for dealing with UXBs. It was found that powerful electro-magnets, 'clock-stoppers', would stop the clockwork fuses, so they could be removed more safely. Then the enemy developed the 'Zus 40', booby-trap fuses that would trigger if disturbed. It was found that dental cement would jam them. The Bomb Disposal Squads would carefully dig them up, then carry them away to a safe place, often driving through heavily populated areas in their trucks with distinctive red markings on the edges of their wings.

The Germans countered this with the 'No.50', an anti-handling fuse where as little as 1.5mm of movement would trigger the fuse. The antidote to this was a conductive liquid, which, when pumped into the bomb, slowly drained the energy from the batteries running the sensors. So, in January 1943 the first 'Y' fuses were used, this time with mercury switches that triggered the bomb at the slightest movement. The answer was liquid oxygen to freeze the batteries. [18]

On 11 April 1944 ten 50kg phosphorous bombs and 111 SD 10kg anti-personnel bombs fell in fields at Menheniot near Liskeard. Ninety-one of the latter failed to explode. [19] This marked a change of tactic in response to our carpet bombing of German cities; now the civilian population was the target. SD2 'Butterfly Bombs' were small; each one looked like a cocoa tin from which two little wings sprouted. The odd-looking devices floated to the ground and if they were touched or kicked by the unwary or inquisitive, then... Fortunately their full potential was never realised, for they could be dropped in large numbers, and would cause severe disruption for some time while they were dealt with. When the Germans tried them out during a raid on Grimsby it took two weeks to clear the 2700 butterfly bombs. News of this was censored. However, talks were given in Cornish schools warning of the dangers of these devices. [20] Fortunately the disruption and fear caused did not filter back to the enemy, who failed to capitalise on these nightmare contraptions. (It was left to the Americans to develop the idea after the war, and then use them in Vietnam.)

In a total of 420 distinct raids on Cornwall, over 19 794 bombs were recorded as having been dropped, of these 518 were UXBs. [21] This figure compares with some 50 000 for the whole of Britain.

During the night of 30/31 May 1944 Falmouth suffered one of the worst air raids on Cornwall. Twenty-five high-explosive bombs, 23 incendiary bombs and 20 butterfly bombs fell on the town. The Pentargon Hotel was demolished and a number of other hotels and properties 'received substantial damage'. [22] Three people were killed and 17 injured. The records explain that:

In the early hours of the morning ... a serious and widespread raid occurred on the town and vicinity of Falmouth. A direct hit on a million-gallon oil storage tank at Swanvale set the spirit on fire and it continued to burn for about twenty-two hours. [23]

Pentargon Hotel in Falmouth was severely damaged during the night of 30/31 May 1944 in what was to be the last aircraft air raid in Britain.

GEORGE ELLIS COLLECTION

Blazing fuel flowed from the ruptured tanks and threatened to engulf nearby houses. Chief Boatswain's Mate Philip Lee Bishop, of the US Naval Reserve, used a bulldozer to divert the flow into a pit, as firemen sprayed water onto the vehicle and driver. For his bravery he was awarded the BEM (military) and the US Navy and Marine Corps medal. [24]

It was to be Falmouth's last air raid – in fact the last aircraft air raid in Britain as opposed to V-1 and V-2 attacks. In 1944 Plymouth was the target for a handful of V-1 attacks mounted from a launch site on the Cherbourg Peninsula. Details of the attack on Falmouth, and many others, were kept obtuse in the local press, or more usually not mentioned at all, because they were subject to a Government D Notice. So unless people were directly involved, they were probably unaware of raids (or casualty rates) in other towns, for after all 'careless talk costs lives'. This prevented panic, demoralisation or social unrest.

As indiscriminate raids in Cornwall increased during 1941 it was not surprising that some of the evacuees wondered what they were doing here when they found themselves being bombed or hiding in shelters. One such raid occurred in November of that year, though in the newspaper report the details of the location were deliberately vague;

There was a direct hit on some houses and another on a cottage a short distance away…

In one house, Mr Charles Bird, a member of the village Home Guard, and his wife were killed. Next door ten-year-old Marion Rickard met a similar fate…

Careless Talk Costs Lives (below left). *Promoting evacuation from the capital. However, this did not guarantee one's safety* (below).

PUBLIC RECORD OFFICE

The fourth fatally injured was Alec Hamilton, aged twelve, who, with his parents and two sisters, lived in the cottage after being evacuated from London. [25]

It is therefore not surprising that the Government Evacuation Scheme's 'Register of Billets and Check Record of Post Office Weekly Payments' [26] (3/- per child; 5/- for an adult) contain many entries for evacuees who returned home.

The indiscriminate nature and often tragic consequences of aerial bombing was perhaps not appreciated at the start of the war. All the country had been divided into 'neutral', 'reception' or 'evacuation' areas. Cornwall was scheduled for reception, yet remarkably Plymouth was not an evacuation area. This did not stop families in the cities unofficially sending youngsters to the safety of relatives or friends at the outbreak of hostilities or as the blitz intensified.

Besides having to put up with homesickness, unfamiliar faces and surroundings, not to mention air raids, conditions for evacuees varied enormously. For some children it was a wonderful adventure, a prolonged school trip. G.W. Pitts, the Headmaster of Campbell Street School, wrote to the *Royal Cornwall Gazette*:

> Campbell Street School, 240 strong, is split up into six groups; at Fowey, Tywardreath, Biscovey, Bugle, Charlestown and Mevagissey. In each of these centres the children have had what surely must be the busiest and happiest Christmas and New Year in their experience. The fun has been fast, furious and continuous.
>
> In every section, the organisers have nobly succeeded in giving to the children a right royal time, and my pen simply fails to do justice to their overwhelming generosity.

He concluded:

> I therefore trust that this expression of our deep appreciation will be accepted by all as an earnest of our gratitude. Campbell Street School salutes Cornwall. [27]

Nowhere did it mention where Campbell Street School was to be found. It was, however, in Paddington, London. Campbell Street School opened in 1881 as a mixed-infant and primary board school run by London County Council. However, the area was re-developed between 1961 and 1972, during which time Campbell Street itself was demolished. In 1962 the school's name was changed to Paddington Green Primary School. [28] Three elderly Charlestown gentlemen, classmates of the evacuees, recall that many of the visitors had never seen a cow before they came to Cornwall.

Campbell Street School was one of four or five schools in the borough of Marylebone that had travelled on 'one long special train', [29] arriving at St Austell station on the afternoon of Friday, 30 August 1939. The group of over 500 children were some of the first evacuees to arrive in the county. 'They all had hand luggage – attache cases, small suitcases, parcels, packages of food, and raincoats – and each one had a gas mask slung over the shoulder. Each one was labelled, and their teachers each wore on the sleeve a white band bearing the letters "L.C.C." [London County Council] or numbers corresponding to the school and district.' [30] One of the boys, feeling homesick on that first night, had cried, 'We've had to come here all because of one man – Hitler.' [31]

Campbell Street School evacuees enjoying themselves on Readymoney Beach, Fowey, on 15 September 1939 (opposite top). The evacuees included the Stevens family. From left to right are Mrs Stevens; Alice (14); Sydney (11); Joan (9); John (7); Raymond (5); George (3) and Dorean (15 months) (opposite bottom).

GEORGE ELLIS COLLECTION

Locations were usually deliberately vague in newspaper reports, but Campbell Street School was in Paddington, London. The school is now called Paddington Green Primary School, but the street no longer exists.

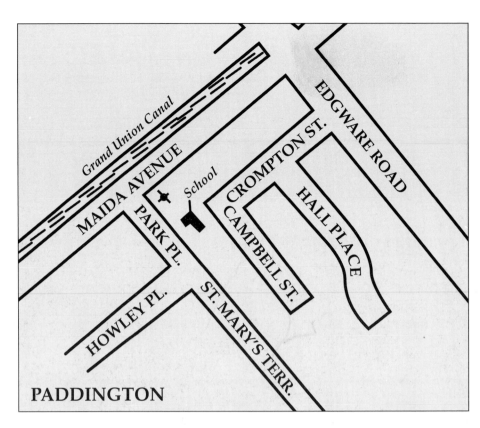

So what was the nature of the entertainment provided which did so much to raise their spirits? The group of evacuees from Paddington who were staying in Fowey at the time were treated to Christmas parties in the Grammar School, one provided by the Freemasons of Fowey, while Fowey Girl Guides organised another one when Father Christmas gave them all presents. They also visited the Troy Cinema in the town to see the film *No Limit* featuring George Formby. [32]

In Truro similar Christmas entertainment was laid on by Truro City Council Evacuation Committee:

> It was decided that there should be a free film show, probably on New Year's Day, to which evacuee children and Truro children will be invited. The children will be given Christmas fare if the rationing problem can be overcome. [33]

Others had a similar time, though the entertainment was somewhat different:

> Two hundred more Canterbury public schoolboys came to Par Station on Thursday, and set out on the four-mile walk to the Carlyon Bay Hotel, Crinnis, their home now until the war ends. They carried light lugguage – their gas masks, tennis rackets and even golf clubs. There is a fine course near the hotel. Heavy luggage followed on lorries. [34]

One of the pupils also recalls making regular rail journeys from Par to Newquay to go surfing. At the time they did not experience any restrictions on these excursions and the boys were able to enjoy riding the waves with makeshift boards, but without the benefit of wet suits. [35]

Besides leisure facilities, the hotel soon sported school rooms and a chapel was created in the large garages opposite. The servants' quarters also became classrooms. The junior school of about 150 pupils was housed in the Cliff Head Hotel, while the choir school was at St Blazey. (Also see Chapter 9.)

The Carlyon Bay Hotel and its grounds, dramatically photographed in 1947. To the rear of the hotel the garages can be seen, while behind the tennis courts on the left is the Cliff Head Hotel. The golf course extends away to the right.

SIMMONS AEROFILMS

King's School from Canterbury, in front of the Carlyon Bay Hotel, St Austell, 23 July 1943. Their cups are proudly displayed before them.

GEORGE ELLIS COLLECTION

For others accommodation was less salubrious, as Gordon Finn recalls. Evacuated from Plymouth at the age of seven, the holiday he had been promised turned into 'another kind of porridge', as he was forced to share a bed with five others in cramped and squalid conditions. Arriving at the Great Western Hotel, Newquay, the first night they slept on camp beds. Then local people were given the choice of the 350 children who had come from London as well as Plymouth. Some found themselves with kind and caring hosts, others did not fare so well. [36] There is also evidence that local people were far more prepared to take in girls than boys. [37]

Part of the problem was that not everyone wished to take in evacuees, but they had little choice. There was tremendous social pressure on people to put up evacuees, whatever the discomfort or inconvenience. In March 1940 it was reported that:

> Mr L.A. Hannuy, evacuation officer for SW England stated, 'The department will expect you [the local authorities] to use your full compulsory powers, with regard to billeting. The roll of householders you will make will probably get you the number of billets required, but if not you will have to use your compulsory powers, and you may also have a little over-crowding to get the children in.' [38]

If this was not enough, newspaper articles such as this one of the following year hammered home the message:

> People with house room who cannot be bothered to take evacuees are like people who stand unheeded on a river bank when someone is shouting for

help. The world condemns them not because they are cowards but because they are inhuman. There are risks, of course, about diving into the river. One may also find the drowning person to be quite unlikeable. But these doubts do not deter the resolute rescuer. [39]

Strong words indeed, but ones that were likely to tug at people's consciences and quell any doubts in waivering minds. Soon billets ranged from small cottages to hotels and country houses like Lanhydrock near Bodmin that housed a group of youngsters from St Joseph's School, south London.

The number of children involved certainly created problems for the local authorities;

The problems arising out of the necessity to find school accommodation for 25 000 evacuated children now in Cornwall was discussed by the County Education Committee at Truro on Thursday … the chief difficulty was lack of school equipment. The Committee decided to ask the Cornish Members of Parliament to press the Government to release more cement for the construction of school air-raid shelters. [40]

Even if their lodgings were acceptable, evacuees faced other problems, including an unfamiliar dialect, customs and Cornish insularity. Ricky Clitheroe, who was just four when he was evacuated from Islington to Newlyn noticed that, 'Cornish people speak very fast and they pronounce their words differently.' [41] The new arrivals were treated with some curiosity, suspicion even, at first. On occasions there was open hostility. 'There were many fights between we Cockney kids and the locals. We were always getting picked on because we were outsiders who were intruding on their territory.' [42]

In a county where few people locked their doors when they went out, the opportunity existed for the dishonest to take advantage of the situation. For example, 'An evacuee woman was charged with stealing another evacuee's suede handbag, shortly after arriving at St Austell.' [43] A month later two evacuee boys were brought before Penzance Juvenile Court, 'for thefts from shops and other places at Penzance, The Lizard, Marazion and Helston, one asked that 40 cases of theft should be considered, and the other 24.' [44] It is perhaps surprising that they were free to travel so widely to undertake this crime spree. One was ordered to receive six strokes of the birch and the other four. The Chairman, Mr G.H. Bennetts noted that, 'there were more than 3000 evacuated children in Penzance, and not all were of a desirable type. He hoped the County Council would realise that it was their duty to provide remand homes.' [45]

Some people looked at such misdemeanours sympathetically and thought there may be mitigating circumstances. For example:

> When seven schoolboys evacuated to Helston were charged at the Juvenile Court on Saturday with thefts from shops the probation officer (Mr B.T. Rawlings) said that the district of London where the boys lived had been heavily raided, and as their school had been bombed they ran about the streets and in and out of shelters without supervision for some time. From information he had received it was quite evident that when the boys reached Helston they were not normal on account of the terrifying experiences they had gone through. [46]

As a result, two of them were discharged, while the other five were, 'placed on probation for twelve months on payment of costs.' [47]

One teenage boy, Ronnie Biggs, evacuated to Medrose Street in Delabole, would later gain notoriety as one of the Great Train Robbers. Mr Norman Amy, who was in the same class as Biggs at school, recalls that he kept out of trouble apart from getting into the occasional fight. [48]

As well as pilfering there were also cases of vandalism committed by evacuees, something that is perhaps regarded as a modern phenomenon. For example, two thirteen-year-old boys were bound over for a year at St Austell, 'for stealing a bicycle lamp, and then breaking it and throwing away the pieces.' [49] Other teenagers were also getting up to mischief, as was reported on the same day:

> Three evacuee boys – two brothers, aged 12 and 13, and another boy aged 13 – were charged at a special West Powder Juvenile court at Truro … with breaking 24 panes of glass, valued at £2, in an unoccupied cottage at Piper's Hill, Shortlanesend, Truro.' [50]

Nor was crime just confined to the male gender, for on the same day it was reported that, 'two evacuee women were bound over for a year at St Austell … one, Mrs E. Allen, on a charge of stealing a push chair, baby's coat and cushion, the other, Mrs D. Galvin, on a charge of stealing a pair of suede fur-lined gloves…' [51] Unfortunately the motives for these crimes were not recorded, so we will never know if it was out of a genuine need for babywear, or just a compulsive habit.

Then there was the unusual case of three evacuee women charged with harbouring an army deserter, after which they were forbidden to allow soldiers to visit their billets at the Barn Hotel, Tregoney (sic). [52]

For some locals, the pressures of billeting evacuees, often against the home-owner's wishes, proved too much, and they themselves ended up on the wrong side of the law:

> An evacuee boy six years old was twice lowered into a well, and was once left there dangling on a rope, it was alleged in evidence given at Penzance yesterday in a prosecution brought by the NSPCC

The defendant was quoted as saying:

> 'Why should we have these kids, these Londoners? I would not have that boy

if he had not another place in the world to go to. He was a cunning, impudent monkey. Why should we have these people foisted on us? They are a nuisance, and killed my ducks before they had been here five minutes.' [53]

Another charge was brought by the NSPCC against a woman at Troon for the ill-treatment and neglect of an eleven-year-old girl evacuee from London who was in her care. [54]

No doubt the evacuees billeted in Cornwall represented a cross section of society, with good and bad amongst them. Some had a pleasant time in difficult circumstances and went on to keep in touch with their foster families for years afterwards. Others, finding themselves in a difficult situation, failed to adapt, or even exploited the situation. For many, hosts and evacuees alike, the experience was to mould their subsequent lives, as well as leaving lasting memories of wartime Cornwall.

CHAPTER 7 – REFERENCES

(PC = Personal Communication)

[1] Winston Churchill in a speech to the House of Commons, 8 October 1940.

[2] *Falmouth's Wartime Memories* (1994), Trelawny, p. 162.

[3] The late Albert Trembath, quoted in the *Cornish Guardian*, 26 April 2001, p. 28.

[4] Ibid.

[5] *Royal Cornwall Gazette*, 14 May 1941, p. 3.

[6] *Fowey at War* (19–), Paul Richards and Derek Reynolds, p. 36.

[7] Ibid.

[8] *When Bombs Fell* (1987), Phyllis M. Rowe and Ivan Rabey, p. 25.

[9] Ibid.

[10] County ARP Records, p. 11, (Cornwall Record Office, Truro).

[11] *History of Incidents, S.E. Cornwall* (Incident No.61), (Cornwall Record Office, Truro).

[12] County ARP Records, p. 11, (Cornwall Record Office, Truro).

[13] *Falmouth's Wartime Memories* (1994), Trelawny, p. 71-79.

[14] County ARP Records, p. 18, (Cornwall Record Office, Truro).

[15] County ARP Records, p. 7, (Cornwall Record Office, Truro).

[16] County ARP Records, p. 8 and *Falmouth's Wartime Memories* (1994), Trelawny, p. 73.

[17] County ARP Records, p. 5, (CRO, Truro).

[18] *Danger U.X.B.* (2001), M.J. Jappy.

[19] County ARP Records, p. 23, (CRO, Truro).

[20] Example in Fowey Boys' School Log Book, 9 December 1943.

[21] County A.RP Records, p. 24, (CRO, Truro).

[22] Ibid.

[23] Ibid.

[24] *Falmouth's Wartime Memories* (1994), Trelawney, p. 68, 70, & 125.

[25] *The West Briton*, 17 November 1941, p. 2.

[26] Cornwall Record Office, Truro.

[27] *Royal Cornwall Gazette*, 10 January 1940, p. 1.

[28] PC: Ms Llinos Thomas, City of Westminster Archives Centre.

[29] *Cornish Guardian and Cornwall County Chronicle*, 7 September 1939, p. 6.

[30] Ibid.

[31] Ibid.

[32] *Fowey at War* (19–), Paul Richards and Derek Reynolds, p. 36.

[33] *Royal Cornwall Gazette*, 18 December 1940, p. 3.

[34] *Royal Cornwall Gazette*, 5 June 1940, p. 2.

[35] PC: Mr R.A. Bedingfield.

[36] *Another Kind of Porridge* (2001), Gordon Finn.

[37] *Royal Cornwall Gazette*, 14 May 1941, p. 3.

[38] *Royal Cornwall Gazette*, 6 March 1940, p. 2.

[39] *Royal Cornwall Gazette*, 23 April 1941, p. 3.

[40] *Royal Cornwall Gazette*, 23 October 1940, p. 4.

[41] *Away From the Bombs* (1990), Richard Clitheroe, p. 7.

[42] Ibid. p. 10.

[43] *Royal Cornwall Gazette*, 30 October 1940, p. 3.

[44] *Royal Cornwall Gazette*, 27 November 1940, p. 5.

[45] Ibid.

[46] *Royal Cornwall Gazette*, 18 December 1940, p. 2.

[47] Ibid.

[48] PC: Mr N. Amy.

[49] *Royal Cornwall Gazette*, 13 November 1940, p. 3.

[50] *Royal Cornwall Gazette*, 13 November 1940, p. 4.

[51] Ibid.

[52] *Royal Cornwall Gazette*, 5 March 1941, p. 1.

[53] *Royal Cornwall Gazette*, 19 February 1941, p. 3.

[54] *Royal Cornwall Gazette*, 26 November 1941, p. 3.

'THE 49TH STATE'

Why, when I was here last time we were quite alone, desperately alone... We were poorly armed. We are not so poorly armed today...

CHURCHILL [1]

One victim of the Battle of the Atlantic was the Dutch tanker Lucretia. *She was torpedoed by a U-boat about 200 miles west of the Isles of Scilly on 7 July 1940 whilst transporting a cargo of gas oil from Aruba in the Caribbean to Avonmouth. An Anson of 217 Squadron from St Eval spotted the stricken vessel. Two crew members were killed but thirty were rescued.*

The year 1941 started on a low with a sense of struggle and isolation, but ended optimistically in the company of a powerful ally. As a result of both national and international events, Cornwall would find itself even more embroiled in the war effort.

Soon after the fall of France the Germans had established U-boat bases on the Atlantic seaboard at Bordeaux, La Rochelle, St Nazaire and Brest, along with a U-boat headquarters at Lorient. From these bases they mounted attacks on the convoys bringing Britain vital supplies from the Empire and the USA. The Battle of the Atlantic was waged between the German wolf-packs of U-boats and the merchant convoys. However, there were rarely enough warships to escort them, and air cover could only reach so far out into the vast grey Atlantic.

Cornwall's geographical location, like an arm reaching out into this ocean, made it ideal for the establishment of forward bases. During the war the airforce was divided into four specific commands: Fighter Command, Bomber Command, Coastal and Training. To these were added Tactical Air Forces in 1943. Each command was represented in the Duchy.

Perranporth Airfield was ready for mounting operations by April 1941 using single-engined fighters. It had been necessary to take over Cross Coombe Farm and to level some of the spoil heaps from Wheal Patience during its construction, but it was possible to utilise some of the buildings of Cligga Mine. The main runway was 1200 yards long, augmented by two smaller ones in a standard A-shaped layout. It also boasted a perimeter track, dispersals and 'blister' hangars.

Number 66 Squadron, using Spitfires equipped with long-range tanks, arrived from bomb-damaged Exeter to fly on coastal defence operations, as well as escorting convoys. By the time the base was demoted to a care and maintenance role in September 1944, some 24 different squadrons had operated from the airfield, including Polish (302 and 317), Free French (329, 340 and 341), Czech (310), RAAF (453) and RCAF (412) squadrons. They all flew Spitfires of various types. Three Fleet Air Arm squadrons also used it in 1944 after it was transferred to 19 Group, Coastal Command. In the three years of use some 80 Spitfires from the base failed to return.

Every pilot's fear was being unable to nurse a damaged aircraft back to base. Operations were often flown well out over the Atlantic or Bay of Biscay, searching for U-boats. If a plane had to ditch in the sea it could be a long wait before help arrived. One Spitfire pilot from 602 Squadron survived on his rations for nearly two weeks before being rescued. [2] Aircraft operating over the sea kept an eye out for anyone who had ditched. To help make it easier to spot airmen in the water the Mae Wests emitted a green dye. If the weather was kind a 'Thornaby' bag could be dropped near the dinghy. However, these had a tendency to drift away from the survivors, or might burst open on impact with the sea.

As a result, the Lindholme dinghy was developed. This could be carried in the bomb bays of search aircraft. Attached to the rescue dinghies were three cylinders on the ends of ropes that paid out for over 100 metres, giving the weary airmen something to grab hold of. Later, larger planes such as Warwicks were equipped with lifeboats which could be parachuted down to a waiting crew. These rescue craft were more like sailing dinghies, and indeed were provided with a sail as well as a survival kit. Some managed to cover large distances before the crews were rescued.

A detachment of a specialised Air Sea Rescue Unit, A-Flight of 276 Squadron, operated out of Portreath from October 1941 and from Perranporth from October 1942. They used the Walrus, an amphibious bi-plane, later to be augmented by Sea Otters. Once a downed crew had been located, a Lysander would drop a dinghy and survival equipment, while they waited for a Walrus to arrive. Specially modified Spitfire ASR 11Cs were also used to drop smoke floats and a dinghy. Air Sea Rescue Hudsons operated from Davidstow from January to March 1944, while RAF Air Sea Rescue launches operated out of harbours such as Padstow. Such units saved hundreds of lives during the course of the war.

When Portreath opened in March 1941 it was used for convoy patrols. Like its satellite, Perranporth, the airfield was constructed on a plateau above the village and overlooked the north coast. In May 1941 it became an advanced base for bomb attacks on French ports. Blenheims of 2 Group were used for this. They were escorted by Spitfires of 130 and 313 Squadrons, who also continued to escort convoys. At this time 'precision-bombing' was being undertaken. Ports, munitions factories and industrial complexes were the focus of such raids. Assessing the success of bombing raids undertaken from bases throughout Britain, an enquiry in September 1941 came to the disturbing

conclusion that only one bomber in ten was getting within five miles of the target! With mounting losses of both planes and crews, bombing operations were therefore temporarily suspended.

In the autumn of 1941 Britain's prospects were looking bleak. The country, fighting alone, risked starvation as U-boat attacks continued to take a heavy toll on the convoys. Added to this came the disastrous news of the sinking of HMS *Ark Royal* in November, along with Rommel's renewed offensive against the Eighth Army in North Africa. The Navy was suffering serious losses in the Mediterranean, while Malta was under heavy attack.

Then, at a stroke, the situation changed. In an unannounced and unprovoked move, in the early hours of Sunday, 7 December, the Japanese attacked the American naval base of Pearl Harbor in Hawaii. The American President, F.D. Roosevelt, declared:

> Yesterday, December 7, 1941 – a date that will live in infamy – the United States of America was suddenly and deliberately attacked by naval and air forces of the empire of Japan... I asked that the Congress declare that since the unprovoked and dastardly attack a state of war has existed between the United States and the Japanese Empire. [3]

Despite being on the other side of the world, this event was to have dramatic repercussions for Britain, and not least for Cornwall. With Germany and Italy declaring war on the USA on 11 December, Britain was no longer fighting evil alone. The first American GIs (named after the General Issue kits which they carried) arrived in Belfast on 26 January 1942, and in Cornwall in May 1943. It would not be long before some locals were describing the county – and Falmouth in particular (see map on page 110) – as the 49th State. (Alaska and Hawaii would be admitted to the Union as the 49th and 50th states respectively in 1959.)

A wartime postcard from the Photocrom 'Fighters & Bombers' series showing a watercolour by C.W. Smith of a Lockheed Hudson general reconnaissance bomber. On the reverse of the card is a quote from the prime minister: 'This is a time for everyone to stand together, and hold firm!'

FALMOUTH AT WAR – Key to Map

1. Tregwynt Hotel – Fort 1 (HMS *Forte*) – British naval base and Admiral's H.Q.
2. Imperial Hotel, Bar Road – Fort 2 (HMS *Forte II*)
3. Town Quay Chambers (above Taylor's Garage) – Fort 3 (HMS *Forte III*) – Offices for shipping and contraband control.
4. Coastlines Wharf, Boyers Cellars – Fort 4 (HMS *Forte IV*) – Motor launches and MTBs.
5. Hydro Hotel, Cliff Road – HQ for Advanced Amphibious Forces and 97 Seabees (Construction Battalions).
6. The Pendower, Sea View Road – RAF control centre for barrage balloon sites.
7. 'Holyrood', Wood Lane – Camp reception station.
8. The Greenbank Hotel – Billet for American officers.
9. 'Lynhurst', Sea View Road – HQ for anti-aircraft defences.
10. Madeira Hotel, Cliff Road – Army.
11. Gyllyngdune Hotel, Melvill Road – Wrens and RN personnel.
12. Pentargon Hotel, Cliff Road – Wrens and Army personnel.
13. 'Holmlea', Cliff Road – Wrens and Army personnel.
14. Carthion Hotel, Cliff Road – Wrens' base.
15. St Michael's Hotel, Stracey Road – US Naval Hospital.
16. Treslothan Hotel, Spernen Wyn Road – Wrens.
17. Arwenack Manor House, Grove Place – Air-Sea Rescue crews.
18. Royal Cornwall Sailors' Home, Grove Place – Relief hospital for British sailors.
19. Ponsharden Lodge – Boat crews for harbour and river launches.
20. Grove Place – Workshop and landing hard.
21. The Beacon – US Camp for American Advanced Amphibious Base ('Seabees') – 1944.
22. Falmouth Hotel, Cliff Road – High ranking officers in transit, finance and US Field Workshops.
23. The Hornworks – Royal Observer Corps.
24. Harvey's Yard, Bar Road – US stores.
25. Ponsharden Shipyard – Servicing Motor Torpedo Boats (MTBs) and Motor Launches (MLs).
26. Maenheere Hotel, Grove Place – Dutch navigation school.
27. Bay Hotel, Cliff Road – Convalescent home for disabled servicemen and Pendennis Battery Plotting Room adjacent.
28. South Cliffe Hotel, Cliff Road – Merchant Navy officers, Wren officers, and sick bay for Wrens.
29. The Gwendra Hotel, Cliff Road – HQ for RAF, control for rescue motor launches and flying boats when using Carrick Roads.

A Wellington IC of 221 Squadron from St Eval flies over a dingy containing the German crew of a downed Focke-Wulf Kondor; 23 July 1941.

The US 29th Division, comprising of over 30 000 men, had arrived in Britain in October 1942 on board the *Queen Elizabeth* and *Queen Mary*, and were transferred to Devon and Cornwall the following May. Bude was soon to play host to the newly-formed 29th Ranger Battalion, while the 115th Combat Team, comprising of infantry and artillery, were stationed in Bodmin and Launceston. Soon other troops were pouring into the county; the 175th Combat Team were transferred to St Ives, Penzance, Camborne and Helston from Devon and would soon be training on Bodmin Moor, an experience that many of them would loathe.

In fact the arrival in Cornwall of American GIs was to be a culture shock for both parties. They might have spoken the same language (almost) but the often brash, open and seemingly well-off and well-equipped Americans, with their ready supplies of nylon stockings, chewing gum and Hershy bars, were at odds with the insular and reserved Cornish, suffering from wartime austerity. It was not long before the 'Yanks' were shipping over their own superior supplies, including canned food, clothing and equipment.

The author recalls a visit to the naval base at Pearl Harbor where an audio-visual display amusingly stated that the war began in 1941. This was not true, even for the Americans, who had by then suffered significant losses, but it does reflect the 'We'll get the job done' attitude of the Americans when they entered the war and arrived on our shores, and allowed Churchill to say that he could finally get a night's sleep.

Not that they were the only foreign servicemen in the county. As has been seen, Commonwealth, Free French and Polish pilots played their part alongside the RAF. The Royal Netherlands Navy was using Enys House near Penryn as a cadet college after the estate had been requisitioned by the Admiralty in June 1940. Any doubts about its future were quashed when the Japanese overran the Dutch East Indies, and cadets from Surabaya Naval College were also forced to take refuge at Enys. They stayed there until April 1946 when, with the liberation of the Netherlands, they were able to return to Willemsoord.

On 15 October 1940 Duporth Camp near St Austell became home to a unit of the Royal Indian Army Service Corps, including 25 Animal Transport Company (renamed 25 Mule Company RIASC in February 1941). Originally from the Punjab, they had already been evacuated from Dunkirk or St Nazaire and had since been stationed at Lairg in Scotland. [4] While many kept to themselves, some of their number spoke good English and are known to have fraternized with the local girls. The officers joined in fund-raising activities for the war effort and the units participated in the 'Salute the Soldier Week' parades in St Austell. The mules were stabled in the old Savoy cinema at Truro Road. They presented a curious sight, and many local residents remember the Indian

Indian soldiers leading their mules laden with bales of straw, 1940.
GEORGE ELLIS COLLECTION

soldiers watering them in the stream at Brick Hill near Duporth, giving them large blocks of salt to lick or leading them through the streets of the town. When they marched through Bugle school lessons were disrupted to watch them. [5] The mules often had guns and ammunition boxes strapped to their sides so, it is believed, would have been used to bring supplies to forward positions, as well as for personal transport.

Sadly three of the Indian soldiers would never leave the Duchy; during a stormy night in November 1940 a large tree was blown down onto one of the chalets where the soldiers were sleeping. The First Aid party of the ARP and others tried to dig them out to the accompaniment of Indian chanting, only to find that they had been killed. They were buried in Campdown Cemetery, Charlestown, in a traditional sitting position. Their headstones are at an angle to all the others, facing east towards Mecca, while the inscriptions revealingly describe them as a Warrant Officer, Saddler and Tinsmith.

25 Animal Transport Company moved on to Devon at the beginning of 1941. They were replaced at Duporth in October 1941 by 7 Mule Company which had arrived in Britain straight from India in May, spending the intervening period in South Wales. [6]

However, it was to be the American presence which was to have the greatest impact on the county. Soon billets were being established at country estates as well as in large purpose-built camps. Prideaux Place in Padstow was one such historic house, becoming home to the 121st Combat Engineers.

In Falmouth, on the as yet undeveloped rising ground next to Dracaena Avenue, leading to The Beacon, a large camp was created using Quonset huts (big Nissen huts). This would be the US Navy Advanced Amphibious Base. Similar camps sprang up next to the roads leading to Penryn and Helston.

A long way from home. One of the three graves belonging to members of the Royal Indian Army Service Corps at Campdown Cemetery, Charlestown.

On top of the hill above Fowey and overlooking the mouth of the river, the eponymous Windmill Field camp was created. This US naval camp had a capacity of 1000 men, and was the base for the 6th Beach Battalion between December 1943 and D-Day, as well as home to ratings of four Royal Navy Flotilla Groups (521, 540, 542, and 551) from October 1944. Again built from the large, arched Quonset huts, the camp boasted a galley, mess hall and a recreation hut. The latter could hold about 700 people and was used for film shows as well as instruction courses.

American B-24 Liberators of the 44th and 93rd Bombardment Groups used Davidstow Moor, which was designated a Class A bomber airfield. They participated in the bombing of U-boat pens at St Nazaire. The base had been rushed into service ready for *Operation Torch* (the invasion of Vichy-held Algeria) before it was really ready, in fact it still lacked piped water and accommodation! The lack of facilities coupled with the fact that as the highest airfield in Britain and standing in the shadow of Brown Willy and Rough Tor, it was guaranteed to catch the worst of the Cornish weather, meant it was not a popular posting.

Davidstow airfield's control tower – 2001.

Churchill and Roosevelt started planning for the future, even before America's entry into the war. Secret discussions were conducted aboard warships moored at Placentia Bay, Newfoundland. This resulted in a joint declaration, the Atlantic Charter, promulgated on 14 August 1941, as well as furthering their personal relationship (opposite).

Gradually the situation improved. Typical of many airfields throughout the country were the 'Maycrete' buildings that were constructed of brick and rendered with maycrete cement. Their identity is easily betrayed by the external pillars protruding from the exterior walls. Such buildings served as mess huts, gymnasiums or domestic accommodation. A range of hangars were constructed and next to the runways pan-handle dispersal areas were provided for the aircraft, often protected and partly hidden by blast pens formed from earthen banks.

For off-duty relaxation 'All Ranks' dances were held in one of the hangars. These were popular with airmen and locals alike. A blue RAF bus was used to bring Camelford girls to the venue, and there they joined the WAAFs, Americans, Canadians, Polish and English airmen from Davidstow, as well as from other bases such as RAF Cleave near Bude. People attended from the local area and from as far away as Launceston. There seems to have been little

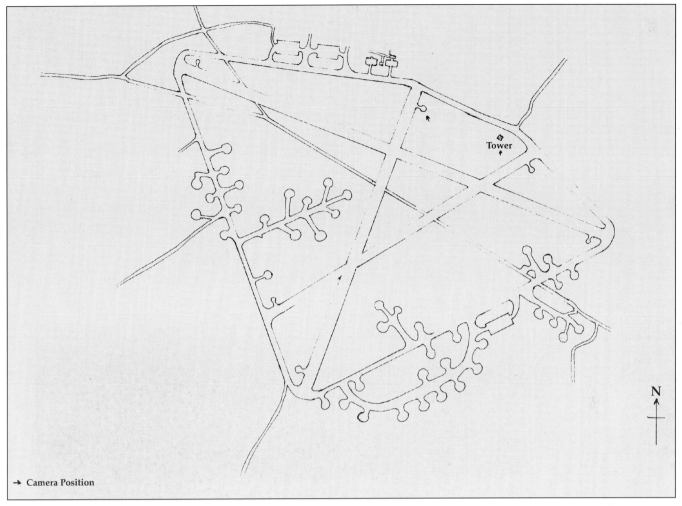

Camera Position

Davidstow. Most of the buildings were at the northern side, while pan-handle dispersals sprout from the perimeter track.

The view from the control tower across the main runway towards Brown Willy and Rough Tor (above).

Looking beyond a surviving dispersal at Davidstow, across the main runway towards Mycrete buildings (above left).

concern about security at the time; everyone was fighting a common enemy. Most of the musicians had been called up, so the band consisted of a couple who had failed their medicals, two women, and Mr Denzil Flew, then a youngster of fifteen or sixteen who played an accordian, and was sometimes joined by a Scots trumpet player. They performed on a stage in the centre of the hangar and the dances went on around them. [7]

American 'jitterbugging' was in vogue at the time. The gymnastic dancing was performed to popular hits such as 'In the Mood', 'Tuxedo Junction', 'String of Pearls', and 'Moonlight Serenade', popularised by Glenn Miller and his orchestra who were undertaking a tour of the country in 1944, including Cleave Army camp. Irving Berlin's 'White Christmas' came out in 1942 and was also popular with American troops during the festivities.

Americans at Tregantle Fort were honoured with visits by heavyweight boxing champion, Joe Louis and lightweight champion, Jackie Wilson, as well as Sugar Ray Robinson between September 1943 and April 1944. Such forms of entertainment helped to boost morale during the heavy training, and at a time of uncertainty and expectation during the build-up to D-Day.

Tregantle Fort, part of the ring of Napoleonic defences for Plymouth. The wooden building in the centre of the photograph was built by the Americans during their stay there.

Operations from Cornwall were not just concerned with the European theatre of war. While fighter squadrons continued to operate from RAF Portreath, ferrying operations grew in importance. In October 1941 a detachment of the Overseas Air Dispatch Unit (OADU) was established there. During *Operation Beggar* their destination was often North Africa, flying south over the Bay of Biscay to Salé in Morocco, so that they could participate in operations in the Mediterranean. Horsa gliders with a crew of three were towed by Halifaxes of 295 Squadron. The undercarriages of the gliders would drop away after take-off. They were then escorted by Beaufighters of 248 Squadron until they reached the limit of their range.

Clearly such operations could be hazardous; on more than one occasion the vulnerable glider had to be cast off and left to fend for itself when they were attacked, and either the glider or the tug was lost along with their crew. In June 1943 a Halifax was shot down whilst the glider ditched. The crew was later rescued by a Spanish fishing boat. In September 1943 it was the glider that was lost, although the crew were later rescued, after the Mk.V Halifax with a single turret, was forced to cast off when attacked by 12 Ju88s. [8]

Operation Cackle supplied aircraft in preparation for *Operation Torch*, then in June 1943 supplied 124 American B-24 Liberators which were involved in the

raid on the Ploesti oil refineries in Romania. Portreath was also a convenient jumping off point for American B-17 Flying Fortresses returning to Britain.

As the focus of the war changed following D-Day, the need for ferrying operations dwindled. The OADU was transferred to St Mawgan in September 1945, and Portreath closed soon after.

St Mawgan had already been used for ferrying operations, being No.2 OADU of No.44 Group Ferry Command. The original airfield at Treblezue, a satellite of nearby St Eval, was inadequate, but by taking in neighbouring farmland and three hamlets, a more practical base was created. By the summer of 1943 the new re-orientated and enlarged runways were being regularly used by Air Transport Command, USAAF. Ferrying operations to North Africa continued, as well as incoming and outgoing flights to the States. In one day, in February 1944, 169 aircraft arrived from America! [9] The base handled an amazing 16 100 movements during 1944. [10] Hotels in Newquay were not surprisingly often under pressure to find accommodation for all the personnel involved, especially when flights were diverted to St Mawgan when other airfields were forced to close because of poor weather.

Following D-Day, St Mawgan was used for training in the use of the new SBS 51 Instrument Landing System. This was provided by the Americans and instruction was conducted by 1529 (Radio Aids Training) Flight. Not that this was the only air training being undertaken in the county. Indeed, RNAS St Merryn's primary function was training. Opened in August 1940 under the name of HMS *Vulture*, it was the only Fleet Air Arm airfield in Cornwall. [11] Two squadrons were based there until 1944: 792 Squadron using Rocs and Skuas to tow targets, and 774 Squadron who were involved in air gunnery training. Basic training was provided and new carrier squadrons were prepared in air-to-air and air-to-ground attacks.

A satellite firing range, known as *Vulture II*, was established in March 1940 at Treligga near Delabole. This was operated by about 20 members of the WRNS. A pair of motor torpedo recovery boats based in Padstow had the task of clearing vessels from the area being used as a firing range. Agricultural land and old quarries near the coast were also used for bombing exercises. Dummy bombs were dropped, then their positions marked to record the accuracy of the bomb aiming. When targets were towed behind planes they occasionally became detached. The local children would make every effort to find and return them to Treligga, for they were usually rewarded for their efforts! [12]

Treligga (HMS Vulture II) *today. Little remains but the solitary control tower in the middle of agricultural land that is very boggy when wet, illustrating one of the problems that faced this under-developed airfield.*

In 1943 St Merryn was developed into the School of Air Combat. This called for the creation of specialist squadrons – 719 provided weapons training, 709 taught ground-attack gunnery, while 175 Squadron specialised in air combat. Seafires from various squadrons were a common sight at the aerodrome.

Further rebuilding began in 1944, and in December the establishment was re-named the School of Naval Air Warfare. This continued to operate in the immediate post-war years.

Like other airfields it occasionally received unwelcome attention from the enemy. At one point the base was attacked six times in under twelve months, culminating in the worst raid on 5 May 1941 when 22 aircraft were damaged and two personnel injured.

Today many people would be unaware that an aerodrome once existed here. One has to look hard to find evidence of it in a landscape of fields and scattered buildings, though a Mainhill hangar survives, along with a short length of runway, dispersals and a few buildings, which have been converted to agricultural use.

Gunnery practice also took place at RAF Cleave, further up the north coast near Bude. A rudimentary airfield on the cliff top, with only a grass runway, tented accommodation and wood and canvas Bessoneaux hangars, it was also blighted by bad weather conditions. G and V Flights of No.1 Anti-Aircraft Co-operation Unit (AACU) were stationed here from May 1939. Westland Wallace biplanes, and later Hawker Henleys (two-seater versions of the Hurricane), were used to release flags or tow drogues off the coast that served as targets. Also radio-controlled 'Queen Bee' drones were used. Experiments to adapt Tiger Moths as pilotless targets had started before the war, but by now they made slow and cumbersome targets, as well as being, one would have thought, a waste of resources. However they did provide the trainees with the experience of a real 'kill' as opposed to shooting a feature-less drogue. The 'Queen Bees' were launched atop a large catapult constructed from steel girders, the plane assisted aloft by compressed air. Facilities at the camp gradually improved, but its location was to ensure that its role would be limited.

St Merryn – guns and equipment being issued to crewmen, April 1943 (opposite, top). Training at St Merryn. An attacking plane flies over the north coast, aiming at the drogue, April 1943 (opposite, bottom).
GEORGE ELLIS COLLECTION

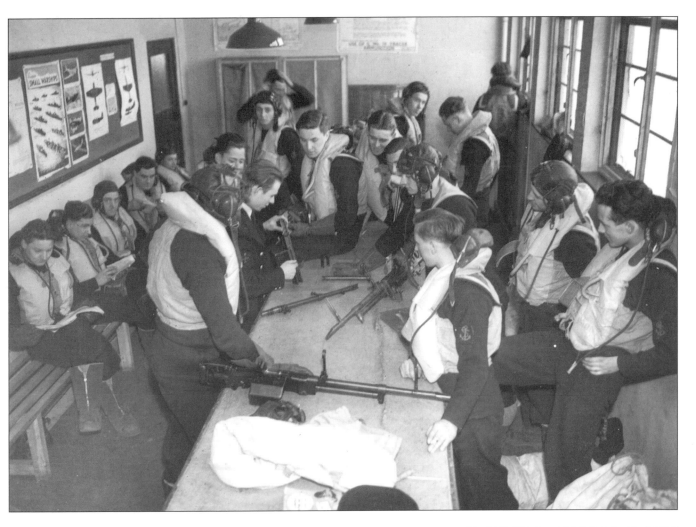

The Drogue Store at St Merryn. The drogues are being folded up for future use, April 1943.

Meanwhile the marine branch of the RAF established the 1101 Marine Craft Unit at Fowey, charged with the task of helping to train air crews in the detection and attack of U-boats. RAF Fowey, as it was known from April 1945, was a Dependent Unit of RAF Mount Batten in Plymouth.

RAF launches, and later a 60-foot pinnace, No.69, were used to tow targets which replicated U-boats. The orginal target, called an Orepesa float, was controlled by cables and could be made to dive as well as emit dye which represented the oil slick from a damaged submarine. These were developed so that subsequent targets even had false conning towers and periscopes. An old Royal Navy steamer, the *Golden Miller*, was pressed into service as a towing vessel. This was augmented by a seaplane tender, ST257, in February 1944 as well as another pinnace, No.50, during April. Planes from St Eval and Mount Batten trained on the targets off the Cornish coast.

Originally No.4, Lostwithiel Street, was used as a temporary store and shelter, but in April 1943 a proper base with accommodation as well as an office, workshop and store was established at 8 and 10 Station Road, conveniently located next to the river where the boats could be moored at a purpose-built jetty. This was later extended by the US Navy and a small Nissen hut was built in the yard behind the base to serve as a mess room. The number of personnel increased from one officer and eight men in September 1943 to one officer and 35 other ranks by July 1945.

Lower Pentire, overlooking The Loe near Helston, was being used to tackle the U-boat threat from a different angle. William Penney (later Lord

A blast pen at St Merryn.

Surviving buildings at St Merryn.

A surviving Mainhill hangar at St Merryn.

Penney) was developing torpedoes here. Once the threat of invasion had passed, The Loe was cleared of defences so it could be used for testing, the aerial torpedoes being launched from antiquated Swordfish into fishing nets stretched across the lake. Their accuracy could then be determined according to where the holes were. Mr Hendy Matthews from Porthleven was employed by the RAF to do this using his pleasure boat, *Isabel*, until the work was transferred to North Wales. The Loe was also used for rocket-firing practice by aircraft based at Predannack. This paid off when, on 1 June 1943, a Beaufighter of No.236 Squadron sank U-418 with four of the still secret new weapons.

The tenacious U-boat crews, disregarding their own horrendous losses, continued to wreak havoc with Allied shipping until the end of the war. Both British and American squadrons had to continue to carry out anti-U-boat sorties; in fact these became even more important as D-Day approached.

Other problems were closer to home. The 1940s were less racially-tolerant times than today. Coloured Americans and whites were often segregated. For example, white Americans were billeted at Hengar Manor while their coloured counterparts were in nearby Camelford. It was even reported in the local newspaper when:

> Many coloured troops of the US Army attended a special service arranged for them in Truro Cathedral on Sunday afternoon. [13]

After a series of fights between white and coloured Americans in St Austell they were only allowed to leave their camps on different nights. However, reports in the local papers concerning wrong-doings by American servicemen are conspicuous by their absence, and no doubt misdemeanours were dealt with through their own official channels and adverse publicity was shunned.

One problem that could not be ignored, however, was the fraternization between Americans and local young women. This reached a point in April 1944 when a statement was issued in the local paper:

U.S. SOLDIERS AND ENGLISH
GIRLS
WARNING ABOUT MARRIAGE

> Many English girls are marrying American soldiers. Many more are seriously thinking about taking this step. [14]

It went on to warn that soldiers needed to obtain permission to marry from their commanding officer or risk being court-martialled, and, '... that marriage will not necessarily entitle them to American citizenship.' [15] If a bride was to return to the States with her new husband '... they may be held up at Ellis Island as aliens.' [16]

It is debatable that many heeded the warning, for many local girls became 'GI brides', and joined some 80 000 who existed nationally by the end of the war.

Clearly after a year of co-existence there was a fascination for all things American. A little over a week after D-Day, on 14 June 1944, Mrs Seymour Obermer, a lady who was 'the wife of an American playwright and visits the States frequently', [17] gave a talk on America at Perranporth. By then all the months of planning and preparation for a second front that had involved so much co-operation, had been brought to fruition.

Chapter 8 – References

(PC = Personal Communication)

[1] Winston Churchill: speech to Harrow School, 29 October 1941.

[2] *Action Stations 5* (1982), Chris Ashworth, p. 146 and *A History of RAF Perranporth* (2000), F.R. Andrew, p. 43.

[3] F.D. Roosevelt to members of the Senate and the House of Representatives, 8 December 1941.

[4] The *Cornish Guardian,* 29 November 2001, p. 31.

[5] PC: Mr R. Sandercock.

[6] PC: Mr J.M. Shapland.

[7] PC: Mr D. Flew.

[8] *Bloody Biscay* (1997), Chris Goss, p. 106-114.

[9] *Aviation in Cornwall* (1997), Peter London, p. 8.

[10] *Action Stations 5* (1982), Chris Ashworth, p. 176.

[11] The only American Navy airfield in Britain was at Dunkeswell near Honiton.

[12] PC: Mr D. Flew.

[13] *Royal Cornwall Gazette,* 8 March 1944, p. 3.

[14] *Royal Cornwall Gazette,* 19 April 1944, p. 3.

[15] Ibid.

[16] Ibid.

[17] *Royal Cornwall Gazette,* 7 June 1944, p. 1.

Padstow's 'Salute the Soldier' parade on 6 May 1944 included these American soldiers. The photographer, George Ellis, tellingly catalogued this as "Yanks".

GEORGE ELLIS COLLECTION

D-DAY PREPARATIONS

I have also to announce to the House that during the night and the early hours of this morning the first of the series of landings in force upon the European Continent has taken place. In this case the liberating assault fell upon the coast of France.

CHURCHILL [1]

There was never any doubt in the tenet of Churchill's speeches that one day, when the circumstances were right, the Allies would attempt to liberate continental Europe. The responsibility for the initial planning of this operation was given to Major-General Frederick Morgan, who had already gained suitable experience whilst planning the invasions of North Africa and Sicily. He was appointed Chief-of-Staff in March 1943, although it was not until December that General Dwight D. Eisenhower was made Supreme Allied Commander. General Sir Bernard Montgomery was appointed to command the 21st Army Group who would have responsibility for the initial Allied ground forces. The title *Operation Overlord* was chosen, and Supreme Headquarters Allied Expeditionary Forces (SHAEF) was established.

The day when all the preparations were complete would be called Y-Day, and this was originally scheduled for May 1944, but later postponed for a month. The day the operation was to take place would be known as D-Day. The final decision for when D-Day would be depended on the state of the tides, the moonlight and, of course, the weather. Given these factors, some time between 4 and 7 June appeared to be the best time.

The decision to invade France in 1944 had been made at the Casablanca Conference in January 1943. By May a draft plan had been drawn up. Of the 2500 miles of 'Atlantic Wall', the focus of the operation was narrowed down to either the closer Pas de Calais, or the area that was most likely to take the enemy by surprise, Normandy. It was the latter that was now chosen.

By January 1944 more comprehensive plans were being formulated, and detailed reconnaissance of the French coastline was undertaken by the PRU, as well as reports gathered by combined operations pilotage parties landing on the beaches, and from members of the French Resistance. This was augmented by pre-war holiday photographs and postcards, after an appeal to the public on the radio.

By now the Germans were convinced that any invasion was likely to take place at the Pas de Calais. This fear was deliberately encouraged by a deception operation known as *Operation Bodyguard*. This would also aim to make the D-Day landings themselves look like a deception to protect a bigger invasion later on, thus tying up German divisions elsewhere. In February a plan was drawn up to facilitate this, code-named *Fortitude*. This was in two parts and with two specific aims. *Fortitude North* tried to convince the Germans that an attack would be launched on Germany through Norway and Sweden, aided by the Russians, while *Fortitude South* would see the creation of a fictitious army group massing to cross the Channel and attack the Pas de Calais. This was given the name First United States Army Group (FUSAG). It was supposed to comprise of 30 divisions. General George Patton was nominally in command, with a fake HQ in Kent. As well as creating a mass of false wireless transmissions to suggest a large military build-up in the south-east, false tanks and landing craft were constructed. Some of these were built from wood and canvas at Boscawen Park Botanical Gardens on the Malpas road, just south of Truro. Decoy encampments were also created next to the Tresillian and Ruan Lanihorne creeks to divert attention away from the real embarkation hards.

In line with this deception, security was tightened. A warning was given in the newspapers that Prohibited Zones were to be set up from 1 April 1944 which applied to '...the coastal belt some ten miles in depth...' [2]

The local paper went on to explain that:

The Secretary of State for War has made the Orders declaring this part of the country protected areas for operational reasons.

In Cornwall the areas affected will be the boroughs of Saltash, Liskeard, Lostwithiel, Fowey, Truro, Penryn, Falmouth, Helston, St Ives and Penzance; the urban districts of Torpoint, Looe, St Austell, Newquay, Camborne-Redruth, and St Just, and the rural districts of St Germans, Liskeard, St Austell, Truro, Kerrier, West Penwith, and the Isles of Scilly. [3]

In other words, virtually all of Cornwall! People who were not resident in the protected areas were prevented from entering them or being there after that date. This was clearly going to be inconvenient, particularly for people travelling through the areas or if anyone was taken ill, so a number of exceptions were granted. Everyone over the age of sixteen had to carry an identity card within the areas. The report concluded: 'Further, binoculars and telescopes must not be used by unauthorised persons.' [4]

Access to Cornish beaches was now restricted, with a £5 fine for infringement by anyone without a pass. Letter boxes were also sealed up prior to D-Day.

It is likely that secret high-powered talks were conducted at Glyn House near Bodmin. Convenient to the Paddington-Penzance line, high-ranking generals and the Prime Minister could be discreetly transported the short distance from Bodmin Road Station (now Bodmin Parkway) to the estate. A fire crew was always in attendance during such meetings. [5]

Glyn House taken from Bodmin Road (Parkway) Station. The house was the venue for high-powered talks prior to D-Day.

There has been some debate as to whether General Eisenhower came to Cornwall. However, it was actually reported in the local papers when Montgomery was in the county in March 1944:

General Sir Bernard Montgomery visited the boys of King's School, Canterbury, evacuated to Carlyon Bay, St Austell, last week-end. Sir Bernard, who was once a pupil in the junior department of King's School, presented to the school the flag which he flew on his car when he commanded the Eighth Army in North Africa...

The enthusiasm and glee of the boys was unbounded at the honour of receiving from General Montgomery the flag... [6]

The report also stated that he had time to stroll in the school grounds and returned to the chapel to talk about his exploits. He 'flew to Cornwall on

Saturday, and on Sunday joined the boys and relatives in morning service in the school chapel, where he read the lesson.' [7] He also inspected members of St Austell Home Guard before leaving by air later that day. It seems inconceivable that he came here just for this visit. More likely, it provided a cover for a meeting on Saturday at Glyn House, and possibly gave him a chance to meet subordinates and troops billeted in Bodmin. After all, D-Day was only a couple of months away.

As for Eisenhower's presence in the county at such a crucial time, this seems unlikely. There is no record of his journey here, and he is unlikely to have moved far from his headquarters at Southwick House near Portsmouth, from where he could stay in touch with Roosevelt and Churchill at any time on secure scramble telephones. Mr P.S. Evetts, who took part in the initial assault as a Lieutenant (E) RNVR in charge of ten LCTs, has done his own personal research into Eisenhower's presence in the county. He refutes claims that Ike stayed at Tullimar, Princess Bibesco's house at Perran-ar-Worthal. The house was used as an officers' mess with cooks, batmen and the like, but suggestions that the Commander-in-Chief arrived there by helicopter – still an experimental aircraft at the time – or arrived in a large staff car, attended by two motorcycle outriders with sirens blowing, seems fanciful. Such stories might have been promulgated as GIs' jokes, or even to deliberately cause confusion. [8]

As well as large numbers of troops being brought into the county, huge amounts of weapons and equipment had to be stockpiled and protected. Convenient locations were found. Stores were concealed in Nissen huts hidden amongst the trees at Lanhydrock, while arterial roads like the B3284, a long, straight highway near Allet between Truro and the A30, were stacked high with ammunition, as well as being provided with cranes to facilitate handling.

For the Allies to invade 'Fortress Europe', they would need to establish a bridgehead. The Germans realised this and expected that a harbour would be the focus of an initial assault. However, learning from the ill-fated raid on Dieppe in 1942, in May 1943 Churchill supported an unconventional idea. Artificial harbours would be created, built in sections and towed across the Channel to a sheltered landing ground. These were code-named Mulberry harbours.

The prefabricated harbour would consist of 213 sections. The largest of these was 61 metres long, 18.3 metres high and weighed over 6000 tonnes. It was stipulated that they had to have a minimum lifespan of ninety days.

When they were finally asembled off the coast of Normandy, five breakwaters were created a mile from the shore using sunken block ships – 'Corncobs' – and 200-foot long ferro-concrete caissons that looked like giant boxes, called 'Phoenixes'. It seems that none of the old vessels which were used as blockships sailed from Cornish ports, though the veteran French battleship *Courbet* was towed from Plymouth on 21 May, via Weymouth Bay, and was sunk on 9 June. [9] On 13 June the *Roebuck* left Falmouth for Selsey to serve as an accommodation vessel while the 'Phoenix' sections were pumped out. These had been flooded and sunk to conceal them and now needed to be made ready.

Within the enclosed area two Mulberry harbours were assembled, A and B. These were to be used by American and British forces respectively, though they were later renamed St Laurent and Arromanches after their locations. There were pierheads of steel girder spans supported on pontoons (called 'Whales') for mooring ships, small craft and barges, and leading off these were roadways, like steel girder bridges, resting on concrete floats ('Beetles') leading to the shore.

A number of 'Spud' pierheads, each with four legs which could be adjusted to compensate for irregularities in the seabed and with a massive floating deck, were constructed at Falmouth Docks, then moored in the Helford River. Several of the caissons were also built there, as well as at Turnaware Point, Feock, and other locations on the Fal. However, the construction workers were not told what they were labouring on – though no doubt they had their suspicions and own theories. In fact various components were constructed in diverse locations throughout Britain, altogether involving about 45 000 workers.

More and more troops arrived in Cornwall as preparations for D-Day intensified. After helping to construct assault training centres at Barnstaple and Slapton Sands, sites chosen because of their resemblance to the beaches of Normandy, in November 1943 the American 254th Engineer Combat Battalion (formerly the 107th) were sent to Newquay. Here they were put through a training programme which included attacking fortified positions, setting up road blocks, crossing rivers, operating landing craft, even using chemical weapons.

During January 1940 trenches had been dug on the hillsides behind the long beach at Pentewan to provide the Infantry Training Centre, DCLI with defensive positions. Now, on 7 December 1943, an invasion force of a different kind was attacking the same beach. The US Naval Advanced Amphibious Training Sub Base (USN AATSB), Fowey, used this along with Crinnis beach for *Operation Number 1*, a small boat landing practice. Officers were billeted at Helligan House. (Here a number of Sherman tanks were left after the war. These were buried in the gardens but later exhumed and disposed of by a local scrap merchant).

Pentewan Beach, used by US Naval units for the training exercise 'Operation No.1' in December 1943. On Blackhead in the background is the firing range used by the local Home Guard. (See Chapter 2)

At the end of the month a three-day amphibious exercise, designated *Operation Duck 1*, was used to practise a full-scale loading by 29th Division from Falmouth, as well as Standard Landing Craft Unit 7 from Fowey. They then had a rendezvous with other units from the South West at Slapton Sands, where they carried out landing exercises. (This would also be the venue for the ill-fated *Exercise Tiger* in April 1944 which was attacked by German E-boats.)

Operation Duck 2, in February 1944, practised using Rhino ferries for the first time. These were large, flat-bottomed barges for transporting men and equipment from larger ships to the beaches. The following month *Exercise Fox* introduced new amphibious vehicles known as Ducks (DUKWs or Duplex Universal Karrier, Wheeled, to give them their correct name). These would become a familiar sight around the embarkation hards of the Fal and Helford. Meanwhile, *Operation Cargo* was used to practise transferring cargo on pallets from Landing Ship Tanks (LSTs).

A joint army and navy exercise, *Operation Splint*, concerned with transferring casualties, was undertaken at Pentewan on 12 April 1944. It was foreseen that those troops who were wounded during an invasion would have to be returned to Britain for treatment. Therefore this exercise involved transferring stretcher cases from small craft, over the sides of LSTs, without stopping to beach them. Designed to carry a variety of cargo to the invasion beaches, from tanks, lorries, jeeps, or even troops with bicycles, it was sensible to then use them for bringing back casualties on the return journey. They were therefore equipped with medical facilities including operating theatres.

In May 1944 LSTs from Cornwall participated in *Operation Fabius*. This, the last exercise before the real event, was also used to practise marshalling the troops. The following month they would be landing on the beaches of Normandy.

Not that this was the only front that had to be considered. To prepare forces for the re-capture of Japanese-held islands in the Pacific, during 1944 Treligga firing range was turned into a mock-up based on Tarawa, a coral atoll in the British Western Pacific Islands (Kiribati). Here tanks – both real as well as replicas – bridges and other obstacles were arrayed to add realism to the exercises.

Sites had to be found where landing craft and troops could be assembled ready for the invasion. A survey was undertaken of the Helford and Fal estuaries, which had the advantages of being secluded, sheltered and offered deep-water moorings. Sites were eventually chosen: Turnaware Bar and Tolverne on the eastern side of the Fal estuary, and Polgwidden Cove at Trebah on the Helford. Underwater searches were carried out to make sure nothing could get in the way of landing craft. Working in secret, over 100 civilian workers were drafted in to prepare embarkation hards. This proved difficult because of the inaccessible locations. However, access roads were built and water supplies brought in. Flexible reinforced concrete 'mats', which looked like the segments in a bar of chocolate, were laid on top of hardcore to provide slipways. Jetties were built out into the water and steel pipes were driven into the river-bed to form 'dolphins'. These were connected by gangways. Jetties like this were constructed at each site.

At Trebah an access road to the beach had to be constructed across nearby fields. This ran down to a gently sloping slipway of concrete matting which was constructed across the entire beach, with a pier extending out from the middle. The woods around Trebah would soon become the temporary home for troops of the 29th US Infantry Division. A sectional concrete road over a

Concrete 'mats' were laid on the landing hards.

kilometre in length was constructed to provide access to the slipway by 'Smugglers' Cottage at Tolverne, and is still in good repair today. The cottage was requisitioned by the Admiralty; the owners, the Newman family, being left with the back of the dwelling while the US Navy used the rest. An observation post and anti-aircraft gun were mounted on the bank overlooking the slipway, with a similar gun on the high ground behind the cottage. A third gun on the hillside on the far side of the river protected the T-shaped jetty and embarkation hard.

An aerial view of Tolverne, showing ships moored in the centre of the river, and the jetty.

P. NEWMAN

A short distance north of St Just in Roseland on the B3289 is an unmarked junction. From here a concrete road runs for over two and a half kilometres providing access to the deep-water mooring at Turnaware Point. The road, although narrower than the one at Tolverne, was also laid in sections, with tar expansion joints between each panel. A broad concrete hard standing was also built behind the beach. The hillside to the rear was bisected by a parallel cutting that was also paved in concrete, creating a concealed area from the access road to the far end of the hard for storing vehicles and equipment. Although overgrown, this can still be explored today. The road is in excellent order, although the concrete 'mats' and the two jetties have been removed. A camp was built at the top of the hill. Units of 29th Infantry Division, V Corps, US Army, left from Turnaware for 'Omaha' on D-Day.

The jetty constructed at Tolverne, reaching well out into the river.

P. NEWMAN

The sections of the concrete road constructed to provide access to the landing hard at Turnaware.

Landing hards were also constructed on the banks of the Tamar at Cremyll for LCTs. A landing hard was constructed at Grove Place, Falmouth, for the repair and maintenance of such craft. Grid-iron piers were also built at Mylor to provide similar facilities. Today this is the only remaining maintenance site in the country which still retains both the grid-iron and 'dolphins', and has recently been scheduled for conservation.

Fowey was one of the main ports in the South West for the loading of ammunition and explosives. They were transferred by rail to ammunition dumps at Par Harbour and Bugle where there were sidings at Carnsmerry and Goonbarrow. The port of Fowey housed a detachment from the USN Advanced Amphibious Base at Falmouth, who used a variety of landing craft, so jetties and moorings were constructed, as well as maintenance and

Is it fanciful to believe that these marks in the road surface were created by tank tracks?

An aerial view of Turnaware Point. The long access road can be seen clearly, as well as the two jetties.

P. NEWMAN

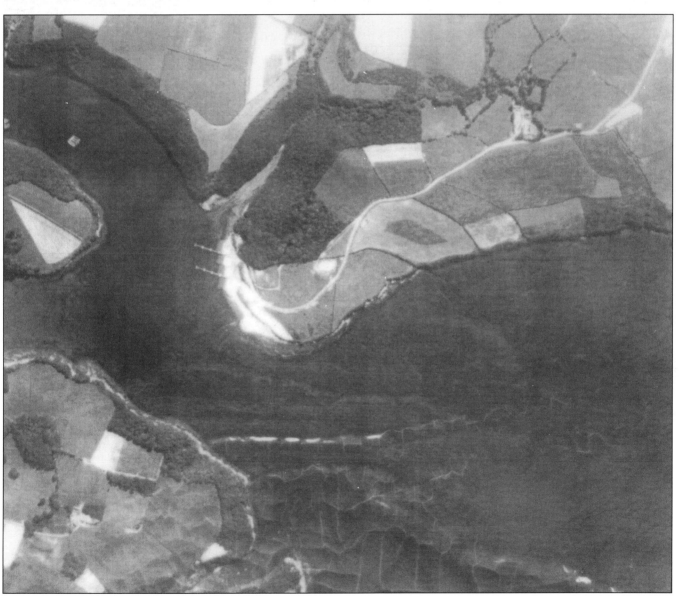

The landing hard at Turnaware Point as it looks today. Little evidence of its history remains.

repair shops. It was natural that it would also be an embarkation point for D-Day.

Areas were also set aside for mustering American troops. One such place was known as H Area. This was in the china-clay district of mid-Cornwall, and ran from H1 on Longstone Downs near Nanpean, through Whitemoor, to H14 at Victoria, Roche. Each area was a tented camp which grew in size as D-Day approached. Then other available sites were utilised throughout Cornwall.

In the east of the county a huge assembly area was created in an area roughly between Downderry, Tregantle Fort and the A38 and St Germans. The Saltash to Callington road (A388) was used as a marshalling area to assemble troops, and became a prohibited zone. Normandy Way – as it was later named – was the route to the ships waiting in Saltash Passage.

The naval aspect of *Overlord* was known as *Operation Neptune*. The combined Naval Expeditionary Force under Admiral Sir Bertram Ramsey, who had commanded the naval forces from Dover which had gone to the relief of Dunkirk, had the task of transporting all the troops and equipment to Normandy. Their destination, Seine Bay, was about 80km long. This was divided into five landing areas, code-named 'Utah' and 'Omaha' in the Western Task Force area and assigned to the American forces, while 'Gold' and 'Sword' were the responsibility of the British, with 'Juno' between them for the Canadians and others in the Eastern Task Force area. Each were then sub-divided into smaller areas.

Clearly air support was going to be vital in the run-up to D-Day. The 150 tugs involved in towing the Mulberries across the Channel, as well as all the landing craft, would be vulnerable to attack. In the preceding six months concerted operations had been undertaken against French road and rail networks to hinder counter-attacks. This was coordinated by Eisenhower from mid-April after he took control of RAF and US Eighth Air Force heavy bombers. Meanwhile, Spitfires from Predannack kept watch over the busy embarkation hards.

By D-Day air supremacy had been achieved over Normandy, although there was no doubt a sense of alarm when planes from St Eval's PRU spotted three German destroyers and escorting aircraft heading for Brest on a course that might intercept the invasion fleet. Beaufighters from Davidstow were scrambled to deal with them.

The first assault ships left for Normandy on 5 June, including the US *Ancon* which sailed from Plymouth to serve as the HQ ship for Force O (Omaha), and the US *Bayfield*, attack transport (APA) and HQ ship for Force U (Utah). In March 1942 HMS *Campbeltown* and accompanying vessels had left Falmouth to carry out the daring raid on St Nazaire. Now a full-blown invasion was being launched. The US *Hambleton* left Falmouth for the Western Task Force area, along with HMS *Vimy*, HMS *Volunteer* and HMS *Boadicea*, although this destroyer later sank after being hit by an aerial torpedo.

Following pathfinder paratroop drops and aerial and naval bombardments of strategic locations, at dawn on the 6th – D-Day – the 115th Combat Team from Bodmin, Launceston and St Austell joined the 116th R.C.T. from Plymouth in leading the assault on 'Omaha' beach. They would meet some of the fiercest opposition of all the landings. LSTs of Force B in follow-up convoys that had left from Falmouth, Fowey, the Helford River and Plymouth now joined the Western Task Force. The first tugs towing the Mulberry sections also left Portland.

On 7 June the APA *Joseph T. Dickman* (formerly the passenger liner *President Roosevelt*) and the passenger/cargo liner *Barnett* returned with casualties to Weymouth Bay and then docked at Falmouth. Yet, 'of 156 000 troops landed by sea and air on D-Day about 10 000 had become casualties, a low figure for such an operation.' [10] Meanwhile, the first 'Corncob' was set up and four Liberty ships, part of a convoy of 34 sailing from the Clyde, called at Falmouth to load vehicles and troops.

Work continued off Arromanches and St Laurent Sur Mer to assemble the Mulberry harbours. The first coaster had discharged its cargo at Mulberry B on 10 June. Then when they were almost complete, the weather, which until now had been capricious, changed for the worst. From the 19th a gale lasting four days battered the Channel coast, damaging the artificial harbours and driving over 700 ships and landing craft on to the shore. It was not until the 22nd that landings could resume at a reduced rate. As a result of storm damage, on the 26th the Americans decided to abandon Mulberry A. The Falmouth trawlers *Northlyn*, *Scomber* and *Settsu*, as well as the *Leonian*, were used to lay buoys and moorings in the Eastern Task Force area.

Some 875 000 Allied troops, 150 000 vehicles and 570 000 tons of stores had been landed by the end of the month. However, not all the American forces were deployed at once; nine divisions were still in England in early July. [11]

Re-supplying the ground forces was vital. *The President* returned from Normandy as part of a coaster convoy to load ammunition at Fowey on 12 June. The tanker *Gold Shell* left Falmouth on 15 June to discharge her cargo at the makeshift facilities at 'Gold' in the Eastern Task Force area, while on 23 June the cable store ship HMS *Holdfast* left Falmouth for the Solent to help to establish a more efficient supply system. 'PLUTO', Pipe Line Under The Ocean, was to provide a fuel pipeline under the Channel stretching to Cherbourg and Boulogne.

Months of preparations had paid off. The Normandy landings had been a success and Cornwall's many billets, mustering points, harbours and embarkation hards had served their purpose and were quiet once more.

CHAPTER 9 – REFERENCES

(PC = Personal Communication)

1 Winston Churchill: speech to the House of Commons, 6 June 1944.
2 *Royal Cornwall Gazette*, 22 March 1944, p. 2.
3 Ibid.
4 Ibid.
5 PC: Mr M. Lyne.
6 *Royal Cornwall Gazette*, 29 March 1944, p. 1.
7 Ibid.
8 PC: Mr P.S. Evetts.
9 *D-Day Ships* (1994), J. de S. Winser, p. 130-135.
10 *Normandy 1944: Allied Landings and Breakout* (1990), Stephen Badsey, p. 42.
11 *Normandy 1944: Allied Landings and Breakout* (1990) Stephen Badsey, p. 48.

'We Will Remember Them'. A poignant reminder that many who left from Cornwall never returned home (opposite, top).

Jeeps would have been a common sight in Cornwall during the build-up to D-Day. Rugged and well equipped – with an axe strapped to the side – they were ideal general purpose vehicles (opposite, bottom).

To Commemorate the D-Day Embarkation June 1944

From Turnaware Beach units of 29th Infantry Division, V Corps, U. S. Army embarked for Normandy early June 1944, landing on Omaha Beach the morning of D-Day, June 6th. We will remember them.

An American Thunderbolt P-47. Although designed as an interceptor, it made an ideal ground-attack aircraft and performed this role during and after D-Day.

RETURN TO NORMALITY

This is your victory! It is the victory of the cause of freedom in every land. In all our long history we have never seen a greater day than this.

CHURCHILL [1]

In many ways the hard-won victory and the immediate post-war era were a paradox. Whilst the war in Europe was over, the fighting continued in the Far East for another one hundred days. Whilst victory was celebrated in an exhausted Britain, war-time rationing continued, or in some cases grew worse. Whilst some celebrated ecstatically, for many triumph was tinged with grief for those who had failed to make it to the end.

By the spring of 1945 people realised that the war was almost over. Hitler's suicide on 30 April was announced by the press the next day and, on 2 May, Berlin capitulated to Allied forces. Germany's unconditional surrender on 7 May marked the end of the war in Europe. With the news came the declaration that the following day would be a public holiday, a Victory in Europe Day.

Peace was celebrated in various ways throughout the county:

There were remarkable scenes of enthusiasm, thanksgiving and rejoicing at St Austell on V-E-Day, when crowds of people thronged the main streets of the town which were gay with flags and bunting. [2]

Pentewan was colourfully decorated for its V-E-Day celebrations with flags, streamers, bunting and electric lights and on Tuesday evening a united open-air service of thanksgiving was held in the Square…

After the service a fire was lit in the Square and a 'guy' of Hitler … was publicly burnt to the delight of all in attendance. [3]

Meanwhile in Liskeard, following the Prime Minister's speech, the mayor addressed the crowds from the balcony of Webb's Hotel. This was followed by well attended church services. 'The celebrations ended with a grand dance in the Public Hall.' [4]

The following week the mayor of Saltash paid tribute to the behaviour in the town on VE Day. He had, '…found no excess of any sort at all in the celebrating of the occasion.' [5]

In the same report, '…the Regional Officer of Civil Defence, directed that the Fire Guard organisation was to be dismissed. The Civil Defence had received word that their duties would cease…' Following street parties in many districts, life was beginning to return to normal.

On 6 August the Americans dropped an atom bomb on the Japanese city of Hiroshima. Three days later Nagasaki was the target of the second bomb. The Japanese Empire called an unconditional surrender on 14 August and the following day was declared a public holiday: 'Victory over Japan' Day. The war was finally over and a renewed outpouring of joy could begin.

VJ Day was widely celebrated throughout the county. In Wadebridge a comic football match was staged, Saltash put on a bonfire, firework display and a fancy dress parade, while in Callington the church bells were rung, a church thanksgiving service was held and there was dancing through the streets. Similarly in Polperro a Furry dance was conducted through the village. 'Dancing and singing continued until almost midnight and a bonfire was lit on the beach.'[6] While in neighbouring Looe, '...a "street" tea was provided for scores of children.'[7] The youngsters also did well in Liskeard for Thursday was declared 'children's day'. 'Each street gave a party for its children and singing, dancing and games were enjoyed. Each street rivalled its neighbour in feeding the children.'[8] Not that the adults were forgotten, for a silver band provided the music for a Furry dance. However; 'Unfortunately the celebrations in Liskeard on VJ night were marred by several nasty incidents.'[9] Some offices were ransacked, and a sailor lost his wallet containing £25 and when it was recovered the money had gone. 'The immediate reaction of the crowd to this despicable trick was to pass the hat around, and £18 was collected.'[10]

Celebrations did not conclude with VJ Day. Street parties and special events to mark the end of the war continued into 1946, although they had similar themes. For example, Padstow's Victory Day Celebrations on 8 June 1946 included a united service of remembrance, water sports in the harbour, a children's tea and fancy dress competition. The event was rounded off at 11pm with the burning of Hitler's effigy and a grand firework display, as well as dancing.

The day after the first atomic bomb was dropped the *News Chronicle* carried the story of the bombing of Hiroshima, 'a Japanese army base'. Beneath the story of the race to create the first atom bomb, it predicted that the energy would in future be used to operate a power plant and that 'CORNWALL HAS URANIUM'. [11] The inference was, wouldn't this push Cornwall into the forefront of the new nuclear age, being a more convenient source of uranium than Bohemia, Norway, the USA or the Belgian Congo?

The chief mineral source of uranium is pitchblende, and the following day *The Times* pointed out that:

> Great Britain's contribution to the supply of pitchblende has always been small, though it … [has] the South Terrace (sic) pitchblende mine, near Grampound Road, between St Austell and Truro, Cornwall…' [12]

A local paper picked up on the story, in their own report adding that the South Terras pitchblende mine was in fact derelict, the production methods employed having proved uneconomic, but:

Now, however with 'this revelation of the secrets of Nature' [quoting Churchill] it seems almost certain that it will soon be working again – and thus a new industry will be brought to Cornwall. [13]

Alas, the dream of Cornwall being in the vanguard of a new nuclear age never materialised.

The war, although difficult and protracted, had not prevented people looking to the future. For many the outcome was inevitable, even if the timing was uncertain; Britain would win in the end. The 'people's war' would lead to a 'people's peace' which would provide better conditions for all. This had been intimated in the Beveridge Report which was widely distributed in December 1942.

There was therefore an element of anticipation and planning for the future. As early as January 1941 the Prime Minister, Winston Churchill, in a speech in Glasgow, had said:

> Do not suppose that we are at the end of the road. Yet, though long and hard it may be, I have absolutely no doubt that we shall win complete and decisive victory over the forces of evil, and that victory itself will be only a stimulus to further efforts to conquer ourselves and to make our country as worthy in the days of peace as it is proving itself in the hours of war.

In December 1941 propaganda film shows were being put on, with the RAF's approval, showing bombing raids over Germany, and similarly books were being published and advertised showing, 'the Empire's Growing Mastery of the Air.' [14]

In 1944 the Ministry of Health was already putting forward proposals for post-war housing schemes, and even considering practical suggestions that local authorities should group together to employ the equipment and labour of large contractors when preparing the sites and road making. This was approved by St Austell Rural Council in May when it was reported that; 'each group of authorities should be able to cope with not less than 2000 houses.' That Council had six sites of five acres or more, and hoped to contribute 328 houses. [15]

Clearly there was likely to be a post-war boom in some industries, such as the building trade. Anticipating this, in June 1944 the Midland Bank was

preparing to support small and medium-sized businesses after the war with 'a far-sighted policy concerning the financial aid they may need.' [16]

In April 1944 the first prefabricated homes (prefabs) went on show in London in anticipation of the post-war housing shortage, due to the number of houses that had been destroyed or damaged, as well as pressures from demobilisation. Several Cornish towns had new estates of prefabs built, such as at Thorn Park, St Austell. Originally intended to provide temporary housing with a life expectancy of twenty-five years, many provided comfortable homes

Prefab designs were simple, but effective.
GEORGE ELLIS COLLECTION

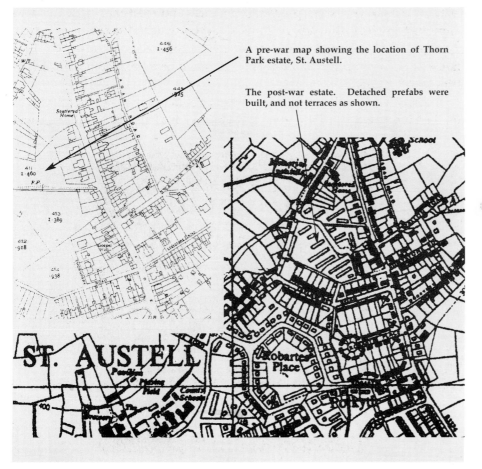

A pre-war map showing the location of Thorn Park estate, St. Austell.

The post-war estate. Detached prefabs were built, and not terraces as shown.

Prefabs at St Austell's new Thorn Park estate under construction on 5 October 1945.

for much longer (indeed, a number at Shirehampton in Bristol still do so today). By 1951, nearly 160 000 had been built.

A local variation was the 'Cornish Unit' which was also seen as a way of quickly increasing the housing stock. Central Concrete Company, a subsiduary of ECLP Ltd, produced them from local aggregates in a similar manner to prefabs, with uniform reinforced concrete sections. Coloured concrete roofing tiles, with the peculiarity of covering the sides of the upper storey, gave the new houses their distinctive appearance. The first one was built in Bugle in 1945, and subsequently many were constructed in towns and villages throughout the South West. In time the dimensions and specifications were modified, but by 1955 over 40 000 had been built. [17]

For individuals wishing to build their own homes the situation was less rosy. Their task was made difficult because many of the raw materials were 'on permit'. Supplies of softwoods, apart from those found locally, as well as steel windows and roofing materials, were rationed.

Despite the cessation of hostilities and the resumption of trade, food rationing also continued on commodities such as meat, eggs, fat, cheese, bacon, sugar, milk, tea, sweets and chocolate. Imported fruits like bananas were particularly missed. The 'Dig for Victory' campaign now became 'Dig for Victory over Want'. In 1947 fat supplies were lower than at any time during the war, and sweets did not come off ration until February 1953 and sugar until September 1953!

Cornwall also found itself with a shortage of miners. As early as April 1944, in a document entitled *Post-War Reconstruction, Cornish Metalliferous Mining*, the Cornish Tin Advisory Committee had advised that:

'...it is abundantly clear to us that unless his Majesty's Government intervene immediately the war terminates, British non-ferrous mining in this country will become extinct. [18]

Cornish Unit council houses being built at Bugle, 2 April 1947 (above).

GEORGE ELLIS COLLECTION

Cornish Units constructed after the war are still a feature of many towns and villages in the South West. These are at Boscoppa, St Austell, but it could be St Blazey, Polgooth, Tresillian, Truro, Falmouth etc. (left)

Prefabs in Newquay being officially opened on 8 July 1946. Mr H.M. Mogford JP, Chairman of Newquay Council, is presiding (above).

Food rationing continued into the 1950s, as evidenced by this ration book dated 1953-1954 (right).

Meat, eggs, fats, bacon, sugar, milk, as well as tea, were still rationed well after the war ended.

With the return of the 'Bevan boys', losses through the casualties of war and insufficient skilled miners returning to their previous occupations, something had to be done to make up the shortfall. The Government remained in over-all control of the mines until 1949 through the Combined War Materials Board. Their response to the problem was to provide Polish miners, many of whom had been working in the northern collieries. A good number would remain in the county; Polish surnames are not uncommon in parts of west Cornwall today.

Not that a lack of skilled labour was the only problem facing the mines. D.B. Barton has noted that; '…war-time conditions of working, rising costs and the labour shortage – as well as the marked lack of success of all the Government-sponsored prospecting – boded ill for the future.' [19] A sad example of this was East Pool & Agar Mine, Cornwall's second greatest tin mine. It had survived the war years through Government patronage, but largely because of a lack of investment was forced to close in 1947. Perhaps its demise served as a warning; in 1948 the Cornish Mining Development Association was formed to try to revive the industry.

Other local industries struggled to return to normality. Like the tin mines, the china-clay industry was experiencing a labour shortage, as well as suffer-ing from a lack of investment and the continuance of out-of-date practices. The number of employees in the china-clay industry had dropped from a pre-war peak of over 3400 people in 1937, to a mere 774 by 1943, although this figure had risen again to 1204 people by 1945. [20]

The war had left its mark on the industry. China-clay production had steadily declined from the start of the war until it reached a trough in 1942 of 175 000 tons, less than a quarter of 1937's production. However, by 1946 the annual tonnage had nearly trebled, though it was still well below the pre-war output. Predictably exports had declined – to 61 927 tons in 1944 – but had risen to 210 896 tons by 1946, though this was only just over a half of the amount exported in 1939. [21]

In addition, there was the difficulty of re-opening the pits that had been closed during the war. Lack of care and maintenance meant that some works had by now suffered landslides or flooding. Yet the incentive existed to tackle these problems; there was a post-war demand for china-clay that was greater than the industry was able to satisfy. In fact, in order to meet that demand it was estimated that production would have to be increased by over 100 per cent. [22] Similarly, the output of Charlestown Foundry increased dramatically to satisfy the needs of the china-clay industry.

In March 1946 a Board of Trade Working Party was appointed, with the brief:

> To examine and enquire into the various schemes and suggestions put forward for improvements of organisation, production and distribution methods and processes in the china-clay industry… to strengthen the industry and render it more stable and more capable of meeting competition in the home and foreign markets. [23]

Their report, published in 1948, recommended the creation of a China-clay Council to speak for the industry as a whole and guide its long-term policy. [24] In fact, an Advisory Board with less influence was established. Following the Government's lead, emphasis was now placed on exports.

Prisoners of war continued to provide their services. Somewhat remarkably, the greatest influx of PoWs into Britain did not occur until 1946. By then there were about 400 camps throughout the country; it being difficult to give exact figures [25] because some were re-numbered while others, like Whitecross Halt Camp, changed from housing Italian to German inmates, and others opened at different times. Bake Camp, Trerulefoot, had previously been home to the American 2nd Battalion, 115th Infantry Regiment, before D-Day. PoWs were used to help clear up war damage and remove beach defences, as well as being engaged in agricultural work. For example, in August 1946, PoWs at Pennygillam were working on the land, while German prisoners at Bake Camp were involved in hedge-cutting, the men working in two gangs, 'each with one man who can speak some English.' [26]

By 1947 there was pressure to allow prisoners to return home, as it was considered important for them to add to the workforce in the western sectors of Germany. Remaining PoWs were repatriated in the spring of 1948. Then the camps, such as at Mylor and Bake, were used to house displaced persons. [27] Today Bake Camp is the site of a sawmill, while those at Pennygillam and Scarne Cross on the outskirts of Launceston have been swallowed up by industrial estates.

Local people were relieved when the beach defences were finally cleared so that traditional summer pastimes could resume. In a report entitled 'Crowded Beaches Again', *The Times* reported:

> The great holiday crowds have taken full advantage of their regained freedom of the beaches at the holiday resorts this week-end – the first August Bank Holiday since war in Europe ended. [28]

Some of the beaches had been cleared of mines, tank traps and barbed wire as early as 1944 so they could be used for training exercises. However, there was still concern about whether all the mines had been removed. At Perranporth the task was not as easy as some might have imagined. 'The problem being of course that the carefully prepared plans drawn up when the mines were laid proved totally useless as the mines had moved along with the shifting sand, and many were found subsequently hundreds of yards away from where they were sown.' [29]

To solve the problem Churchill tanks were fitted with water jets to uncover them. The weapons were then placed in deep pits and exploded in groups, though not without causing damage to property in the village. [30] Finally, it could be reported in May 1946 that 75 mines had been removed from Perranporth Sands by No.7 Bomb Disposal Squad RE. [31]

In October 1945 the guns and equipment at St Catherine's Fort, Fowey, were dismantled by the War Office Armament Removal Party and taken to Pendennis Castle. Beach defences at Fowey were removed by German PoWs. At St Anthony Battery the shells were taken to Grampound Road Station, while the cartridges were dumped over the cliff and later burnt on the beach. The same thing happened at Pendennis Point, where they made an impressive conflagration! [32]

Where, only a short time before, large concentrations of men and equipment had been gathered in expectation of D-Day at Tolverne, now, across the river, British warships were ignominiously moored, awaiting an uncertain fate. Amongst these could be seen HMS *Ajax* which had played such an important role in the defeat of the *Graf Spee* during the Battle of the River Plate in the first year of the war, and firing on shore targets on the morning of D-Day. Others moored with her included HMS *Adventure*, the Royal Navy's first purpose-built minelayer which had been converted to a landing craft repair ship, HMS *Albatross* and HMS *Cape Town*. They had all served in the D-Day landings.

Some American equipment had remained in Cornwall. A number of Jeeps were acquired locally, while a DUKW was given a local registration number, JRL 301, repainted light blue and white, and was used to give pleasure trips from Falmouth.

Remaining munitions were less welcome. The Record of Unexploded Bombs opened with a UXB at Penhale Camp near Cubert on 7 July 1940, but its last entry was not until 7 July 1951 when a bomb was found at Princes Common near St Columb. [33] The record might have closed at that point but UXBs and other ordnance have continued to be found at regular intervals, such as a shell at a residential home in Foxhole in August 2001. Similarly, fishermen have often found mines in their nets. Sometimes these have been exploded at sea, while others have been de-activated and used as collecting boxes for local charities.

Few could have predicted that St Mawgan would become the county's principal RAF station after the war. Nor was its predominance inevitable for by 1947 it had been demoted to a care and maintenance role like many other superfluous aerodromes in the county. It did not gain a new lease of life as a military base until 1951 when the Air Ministry decided to re-open it.

RAF Perranporth had been reduced to a care and maintenance role in May 1945. However, when civil flights in and out of St Mawgan were stopped to make way initially for the fledgling School of Maritime Reconnaissance, Perranporth, now called Trevellas, took up this role and continues to provide a service for light aircraft.

Today Nancekuke is better known for the secret and controversial work that was undertaken there when it was a Chemical Defence Establishment, but this

Wartime shell uncovered

A SIX-INCH long shell from the 1939-45 war was dug up by workmen in the garden of the Melbourne House residential home in Foxhole last week.

The 13 residents and three staff did not need to be evacuated and the shell was safely disposed of.

Cornish Guardian, *9 August 2001.*

Trawler nets wartime bomb

PLYMOUTH Royal Navy Explosive Ordnance Disposal Unit gave advice to Brixham-registered trawler FV Valhalla after she netted an old war mine off Rame Head. The vessel dragged the mine into more sheltered waters. The mine is now on the sea bed at a depth suitable for ordnance disposal experts to dive on it. A spokesman for Brixham Coastguard said: "It has been buoyed off and poses no danger to shipping in its current position. If you emptied the English Channel, you'd find thousands of these devices. It will be dealt with early this week."

Western Morning News, *18 March 2002.*

did not begin at the former RAF Portreath until 1950. More obvious are the large satellite communication dishes now situated at RAF Cleave (Morwenstow) which can be seen from miles around.

Predannack is now used by helicopters from RNAS Culdrose. The naval air station itself, HMS *Seahawk*, was not established until 1947.

St Eval, described in 1942 as, 'probably the most constantly active flying base in the whole country',[34] is now quiet. Today the airfield is dotted with large radar transmitters. Run by the Ministry of Defence, access to most of the airfield is curtailed by a forbidding high chain-link fence and 'Keep Out' signs. Most of the wartime buildings and all the hangars have gone. The isolated church remains as a sentinel to the base's illustrious past.

The Second World War was indeed an international conflict. Cornwall, a remote county of one of the main combatants, played a larger role than many people imagine. Theatres of war in northern Europe, North Africa and the Pacific all influenced events in the Duchy. It also played host to servicemen and women from throughout the Empire and the USA, as well as housing enemy PoWs. In such ways the war opened Cornwall to the world and its pre-war insularity was lost for ever.

Most of the physical evidence of the war may have disappeared, but even people born after 1945 live in its shadow. It is in our psyche, our not so distant past. People live with the knowledge that, but for the war, they may now have another grandparent, aunt or uncle.

A pillbox, now neatly utilised as the base of Pentewan Sands Sailing Club Race Office.

War memorials: the imposing cross at Newquay to those who were lost in two world wars (opposite top).

The memorial in the Square at Pentewan, erected on the 50th anniversary of VE Day. The square was the scene of much rejoicing at the end of hostilities (opposite bottom).

Nor should it be forgotten just how close to invasion we came. The enemy compiled maps of the main towns and lines of communication in the South West,[35] drew up plans of attack and prepared invasion barges. Would we have been able to repel an invasion? Would Cornwall's defences have been equal to the task? Could we have relied on the Army and Home Guard to rebuff the invader? If the Germans had secured a bridgehead, could the Auxiliary Units have used guerilla warfare to mount a successful counter attack? Fortunately, none of the preparations were ever put to the test.

As I write this in 2002 Britain is considering European monetary union and even contemplating a future federal Europe. All this could have been achieved by another means some sixty years ago had not people bravely defended their country, many paying the ultimate sacrifice. To them we owe our freedom, and the chance to choose our own destiny today.

CHAPTER 10 – REFERENCES

(PC = Personal Communication)

[1] Winston Churchill: speech from the balcony of the Ministry of Health, London, 8 May 1945.

[2] *Cornish Guardian and Saltash Gazette*, 10 May 1945, p. 5.

[3] Ibid.

[4] *Cornish Guardian and Saltash Gazette*, 10 May 1945, p. 7.

[5] *Cornish Guardian and Saltash Gazette*, 17 May 1945, p. 2.

[6] *Cornish Guardian and Saltash Gazette*, 23 August 1945, p. 3.

[7] Ibid.

[8] Ibid.

[9] Ibid.

[10] Ibid.

[11] *News Chronicle*, 7 August 1945, p. 1.

[12] *The Times*, 8 August 1945, p. 4.

[13] *Lostwithiel and Fowey Guardian*, 9 August 1945, p. 7.

[14] *Royal Cornwall Gazette*, 10 December 1941, p. 1.

[15] *The St Austell Gazette*, 3 May 1944, p. 1.

[16] *The West Briton*, June 1944, p. 1.

[17] *The History of English China Clays* (19–), Kenneth Hudson, p. 131.

[18] *Royal Cornwall Gazette*, 5 April 1944, p. 3.

[19] *A History of Tin Mining and Smelting in Cornwall* (1967), D.B. Barton, p. 238.

[20] *Board of Trade Working Party Reports – China-Clay* H.M.S.O. 1948, Appendix IX, p. 67.

[21] *Board of Trade Working Party Reports – China-Clay* H.M.S.O. 1948, Appendix I, p. 58.

[22] *The History of English China Clays* (19–), Kenneth Hudson, p. 95.

[23] *Board of Trade Working Party Reports – China-Clay* H.M.S.O. 1948, p. (iv).

[24] *Board of Trade Working Party Reports – China-Clay* H.M.S.O. 1948, p. 54.

[25] PC: N. Hill, Eden Camp, N. Yorkshire.

[26] Letter from Divisional Surveyor's Office, Liskeard, concerning Bake PoW Camp and Operation 'Prisoners', 14 August 1946, (Cornwall Record Office, Truro).

[27] PC: N. Hill.

[28] *The Times*, 6 August 1945, p. 8.

[29] *Perran at War: Memories of Perranporth Pre-War, Wartime and the Late 1940s* (1995), Michael Edwards, p. 43.

[30] Ibid.

[31] *West Briton*, 23 May 1946, p. 4.

[32] PC: Mr A.V. Heggie.

[33] Cornwall Record Office, Truro.

[34] Group Captain (then Wing Commander) F.C. Richardson C.B.E., quoted in *The Memories Linger On – A Collection of Reminiscences of Wartime St Eval* (1989), by Jean Shapland, p. 25.

[35] *Devon at War 1939–1945* (1994), Gerald Walsey, p. 48, 61–65.

A celtic cross provides a memorial on the outskirts of Truro on the cross roads at the top of Tregolls Road (above left).

The elegant memorial in the churchyard at Probus. On the opposite side to those who fell in the Great War 1914–1918 it commemorates those who were lost in the 'Great War 1939–45' (above right).

BIBLIOGRAPHY

Acton, Viv and Carter, Derek *Operation Cornwall 1940–1944 The Fal, Helford and D-Day* Landfall Publications, 1994.

Acton, Viv and Carter, Derek *The Road to Victory – and Beyond – The Sequel to Operation Cornwall* Landfall Publications, 1995.

Andrew, F.R. *The History of RAF Perranporth 1941–1945* Penwartha Press, 2000.

Ashworth, Chris *Action Stations 5. Military Airfields of the South-West* Patrick Stephens Ltd, 1982.

Badsey, Stephen *Normandy 1944: Allied Landings and Breakout* Osprey Publishing Ltd, 1990.

Baker, Arthur *Royal Air Force Fowey – A History of 1101 Marine Craft Unit* Arthur Baker, 1993.

Barton, D.B. *A History of Tin Mining and Smelting in Cornwall* D. Bradford Barton Ltd, 1967.

Barton, R.M. *A History of the Cornish China-Clay Industry* D. Bradford Barton Ltd, 1966.

Bishop, Peter (Editor) *Keep Smiling Through* Brannel School, St Stephen, 1997.

Board of Trade Working Party Reports – China-Clay H.M.S.O., 1948.

Bowyer, Michael J.F. *The Battle of Britain 50 Years On* Patrick Stephens Ltd, 1990.

Buckley, J.A. *A Miner's Tale – The Story of Howard Mankee* Penhellick Publications, 1988.

Clitheroe, Ricky *Away from the Bombs* Richard Clitheroe, 1990.

Davies, J. *The Wartime Kitchen and Garden* B.B.C. Books, 1993.

Edwards, Michael *Perran at War. Memories of Perranporth Pre-War, Wartime and the Late 1940s* Penwartha Press, 1995.

Finn, Gordon *Another Kind of Porridge* Coulmore Press, 2001.

Gardiner, Juliet *The 1940s House* Channel 4 Books, 2000.

Godfrey, Major E.G. *The Duke of Cornwall's Light Infantry* Images Publishing (Malvern) Ltd, 1994.

Goss, Chris *Bloody Biscay* Crecy Publishing Ltd, 1997.

Harper, Frank and Shepherd, Ian *R.A.F. St Eval 1939–1945* New St Eval Memorial Fund, 2000.

Hudson, Kenneth *The History of English China Clays* David & Charles, 19–

Jappy, M.J. *Danger U.X.B.* Channel 4 Books, 2001.

London, Peter *Aviation in Cornwall* Air – Britain (Historians) Ltd, 1997.

Lord, Walter *The Miracle of Dunkirk* The Viking Press, 1982.

Montagu of Beaulieu E.D-S-M, Baron *The British Motorist* Queen Anne Press, 1987.

Nesbit, Roy Conyers *Eyes of the RAF – A History of Photo-Reconnaissance* Alan Sutton Publishing Ltd, 1996.

Pye, Andrew and Woodward, Freddy *The Historical Defences of Plymouth* Exeter Archaeology Fortress Study Group S.W., 1996.

Richards, Paul and Reynolds, Derek *Fowey at War* Cornwall County Council, 19-

Rowe, Phyllis M. and Raby, Ivan *When Bombs Fell – The Air Raids on Cornwall During the Second World War* Ivan Raby, 1987.

Shapland, J. *The Memories Linger On – A Collection of Reminiscences of Wartime R.A.F. St Eval* Jean Shapland, 1989.

Smith, G. *Devon and Cornwall Airfields in the Second World War* Countryside Books, 2000.

Stafford, D. *Secret Agent – The True Story of the Special Operations Executive* BBC Publications, 2000.

Stevenson, Derek Leyland *Five Crashes Later – The Story of a Fighter Pilot* William Kimber & Co. Ltd, 1988.

The Fal Local History Group *History Around the Fal – Part Four* The Fal Local History Group, 1986.

Trelawny *Falmouth's Wartime Memories* Arwenack Press, 1994.

Trounson, J.H. *The Cornish Mineral Industry: Past Performance and Future Prospects – A Personal View 1937–1951* University of Exeter, 1989.

Walford, Eddie *War over the West* Amigo Books, 1989

Wasley, Gerald *Devon at War 1939–1945* Devon Books, 1994.

West, Nigel *Secret War: The Story of SOE, Britain's Wartime Sabotage Organisation* Hodder & Stoughton, 1992.

Winser, John de S. *The D-Day Ships* World Ship Society, 1994.

Winser, John de S. *BEF Ships before, at and after Dunkirk* World Ship Society, 1999.

Young, Martin and Stamp, Robbie *Trojan Horses – Deception Operations in the Second World War* Mandarin, 1991.

INDEX

(Figures in italics denote picture captions.)